A PRACTICAL GUIDE TO FERRET CARE

Second Edition

Published by: **ferrets** INC.

P.O. Box 450099
Miami, Florida 33245-0099

Book design: Deborah Jeans, Jerri Hamrick & Silvia Pease

Logo and illustrations by Monica Lima for Ferrets Inc. Tommy and Twinkle are registered trademarks for Ferrets Inc. and may not be reproduced in any form without written permission from Ferrets Inc.

The Ferrets Inc. Logo: Wheezee: She was perfect, delicate and graceful.

Cover photography: Bob Lasky

On the cover: 1 1/2-year-old Newfy

Cover design: Silvia Pease, Pease Design Inc.

Artwork: Bonnie Bee: pp. 152, 160

Photo credits: Bob Lasky: pp. 17, 24, 25, 49, 53, 56, 57, 81, 88, 89, 92, 93, 113, 129, 133, 137, 148, 152, 160
Michael Riley: p. 17
Deborah Jeans: p. 148

Printed in the United States of America

ISBN 0-9642589-1-9

Distributed in the United States by:
Ferrets Inc.
Phone: 1-800-988-0988 or (305) 856-8566
Fax: (305) 285-6963

Featuring...

Tommy & Twinkle

Little Debbie Jeans with her grandpa Badcock

Dedication

My Grandpa

Augustus William Badcock (1888-1969)

Pop was a quiet, gentle, good-hearted soul who had a great compassion for animals. He raised goats, chickens, a rabbit named Barney, a dog named Rex and many cats and birds. He also sheltered and lost his heart to any helpless or stray animal.

Pop embraced me as a child and taught me about animals; about the uniqueness and special needs of animals, and about the unconditional love, loyalty and respect animals deserve.

I was taught how to safely and kindly hug and pet an animal. I also learned that because animals have feelings, I must always be very careful not to hurt them in any way.

Pop explained each and every thing he was doing and why. For example, as Pop nurtured a sick animal, he would show me how to be gentle, how to speak to it in a soft tone of voice, how important it was to give it medical care, nutritious food and why it needed to rest. I watched as my Pop worked miracles with animals.

I am grateful for Pop's love and support, which will last a lifetime. I celebrate his memory. I invite you to travel with me as I walk in my grandfather's footsteps.

A Special Thank You

Susan A. Brown, D.V.M., for encouragement, guidance and medical editing.

Tsitsi Wakhisi, editor. Her name, which is from East Africa, has created many a question. But her talent speaks for itself. She is managing editor of the Miami News Service at the University of Miami. She previously has held editing and reporting positions at newspapers throughout the Midwest and Florida. When I run out of words, I run to Tsitsi.

Monica Lima, illustrator. Tommy Ferret came easily to Monica. We worked closely together and within four short months Tommy was born. He seemed so alive to some readers of my first edition that I actually received gifts of food and bedding for him in the mail. Twinkle, however, was Monica's nightmare. I could see her in my mind's eye but explaining her to Monica and putting Twinkle on paper were another story. Every part of Twinkle's body was redrawn a hundred times until I said THAT'S IT!! THAT'S TWINKLE!! Monica cried a sigh of relief!

Jerri Hamrick, typesetter. We worked day and night for one year on the first edition. When it was over - she quit! I had exhausted the poor girl, but after a rest, she returned for the second edition.

Thomas Willard, Ph.D., (Performance Foods Inc., makers of the Totally Ferret diet) with more than 23 years of experience in animal nutrition, answered many questions regarding the nutritional needs of the domesticated ferret.

Jan Bellows, D.V.M., (All Pets Dental Clinic, Pembroke Pines, Florida) is one of 30 Board Certified Veterinary Dental Specialists in the world. Dr. Bellows contributed information regarding ferret dentistry.

Bruce Williams, D.V.M., (Armed Forces Institute of Pathology, Washington, D.C.) is a diplomate of the American College of Veterinary Pathologists. Dr. Williams proofread this book and contributed information regarding the dangers of pine and cedar chips and the viral disease Epizootic Catarrhal Enteritis (ECE).

Deborah Kemmerer, D.V.M., (West End Animal Hospital, Newberry, Florida) contributed information regarding heart disease in ferrets.

Susan Erdman, D.V.M., Robert T. Pane, D.V.M., Mary Chavez, D.V.M., Linda Jaffe, D.V.M., for proofreading.

Corey Hoffman, my support system, legal counsel and friend, always believed in this project.

Bob Lasky's work as an artist includes lifestyle, fashion and celebrity photography. Bob's work has appeared in Vogue, People, Teen, Mademoiselle, GQ, Cosmopolitan, Harper's Bazaar and many other publications. Now the domesticated ferret has weaseled its way in front of Bob's camera.

Angela Espinet, Barbara Ludt, Mary Van Dahm, Pam Grant, Ann Davis, Jodi Schroth, Jeanne Carley and Bill Phillips - for being there to answer questions.

Mary Mayday has worked with tamed polecats for many years. She contributed information on polecats and worked with photographer Michael Riley to ensure that we had a photograph of this beautiful animal.

Betsey Zion and Bobbi Snyder, (Copy Express, Miami, Florida) for taking great care of our (Ferrets Inc.) every need even when they are swamped.

Tommy Ferret is named for my brother Thomas William Jeans (1955-1984). As a young man Tom became terminally ill. Yet, in spite of his debilitating health and loss of eyesight and strength, he never gave up. While staring death in the face, he courageously inspired happiness in all who knew him.

To the memories of my ferrets, Wheezee Girl (Without her this book would not exist.) and Pepper Head. (He took great care of Wheezee.). I miss them so.

And last, but certainly not least, thanks to my furry ferret friends, Twiggy Silk and Newfy, my cats... Bando Boy, Kemosabe, Max, Earl Grey and Panda Doll, and Hailey (the world's most adorable dog). I look forward to playtime everyday.

TABLE OF CONTENTS

Chapter 5
HANDLING & SOCIALIZING   69

Chapter 6
HOUSEBREAKING   80

Chapter 7
A GUIDE TO GROOMING   86

Chapter 8
FERRETS & THEIR FRIENDS   106

Chapter 9
TRAVEL PRECAUTIONS 114

Chapter 10
HEALTH CONCERNS 122

Chapter 11
REMEMBERING WHEEZEE AND PEPPER 152

Chapter 12
FERRET CONNECTIONS 162

Foreword

This new, expanded edition of *A Practical Guide To Ferret Care* is the most comprehensive book on the subject of ferrets I have ever encountered. Not only does it present detailed information on the loving care of ferrets, it also offers a valuable source of ferret shelters, associations and products. The book is easy to read because of Deborah Jeans' concise writing style combined with her love of the ferret.

To produce the first and the second editions of this book, the author set aside everything else in her life and put all of her efforts toward gleaning the truth about ferrets from a variety of sources.

Twenty years ago when I started practicing veterinary medicine, most of the available material on ferrets came from Great Britain. The books demonstrated how to keep ferrets for hunting or as experimental laboratory animals.

Articles in veterinary literature often referred to the ferret as potentially difficult to handle and vicious. I remember one article with several colored illustrations showing a veterinarian wearing heavy, leather gloves handling a ferret.

My own experience proved differently. From the beginning, I found ferrets to be tame and easy to handle. In 1982, when one of my clients gave me my first ferret, Lola, I continued to read everything I could get my hands on from our veterinary school library. Because the literature was so scarce, that task took only one afternoon!

With growing interest in ferret ownership, veterinary information started to increase. I began to find some books that were useful, but none that had the detail I was looking for. Almost all still contained at least a few bits of old and outdated information. I still felt there was a void when it came to an excellent and detailed book on the care of ferrets as pets.

Deborah Jeans clearly wanted her books to be complete and accurate. She meticulously has gathered information from many veterinarians, pet care professionals, ferret organizations, shelters and ferret owners. She is not one to be a blind believer in what anyone says; she has to have the facts proven to her, always having the ferret's best interest at heart.

The author also has been an accurate observer of her own pet ferrets throughout their lives. She knows very well what it is to go through those first moments when you bring your new ferret home and the sadness of letting go when a pet must cross the final threshold of death.

I highly recommend this book to both new and experienced ferret owners. Every veterinarian, pet store employee and shelter worker who deal with ferrets should read this book from cover to cover.

I was pleased when the author asked me to be one of the reviewers for the first edition of A Practical Guide To Ferret Care. From that moment on, I have found working with Deborah Jeans to be a joy and a tremendous education.

Susan A. Brown, D.V.M.
Midwest Bird & Exotic Animal Hospital
Westchester, Illinois

Introduction

Get ready for your package tour into the world of the domesticated ferret! This customized journey will take you back in time to the ferret's history and domestication, and you also will learn about the ferret's characteristics and behavior.

As you travel forward you will find many places from which to choose your new companion. Then you will be guided through its essential lifetime veterinary care program. Next, you will visit the ferret's ferret-proofed domain, filled with all of its housing essentials and toys.

Afterwards, be prepared for some social time. In this area you will discover that human ferret parents are not born, they are created on the job! Children will be required to observe the pet-safety guidelines.

Please remain seated in the litter-training area. A slight distraction could cause a ferret "accident".

A raincoat will be necessary for the next adventure because getting wet is where it's at in ferret grooming.

On your next stop, you will be entertained by high-spirited, mischief-making ferrets chasing and teasing their companion friends, the cat and dog. Warning signs are posted - no mice, rabbits, birds or other small animals allowed.

In the travel zone you will learn how to safely travel with a ferret. Preplanning is necessary.

The final frontier prepares you to care for ill and aging ferrets. You will be invited to share my personal journey with Wheezee and Pepper as well as my joys, my growth and my tears.

Tommy and Twinkle are your tour guides.

ALL ABOARD THE FERRET EXPRESS!!

Chapter 1
ALL ABOUT FERRETS

What Is A Ferret?

A ferret is the fun-loving little critter that mischievously has frolicked its way into the hearts of millions. And not only in North America, but throughout the world in countries such as Great Britain, Australia, New Zealand, Germany, Sweden, the Netherlands and Japan.

Despite what some people may think, ferrets are NOT rodents. They are NOT EVEN REMOTELY related to the rodent family. The ferret, a small mammal, is the only domesticated member of the weasel family *Mustelidae* (mus-tell-ih-day). The wild mustelids of this family include weasels, minks, polecats, stoats or ermines, martens, skunks, badgers, otters, wolverines and the endangered North American black-footed ferret.

This family is of the order *Carnivora*, which means *flesh eaters*.

The ferret, a descendant of the polecat, is believed to be a domesticated form of the European polecat *Mustela* (mus-tell-uh) *putorius* (pew-tor-ee-us) or possibly the Siberian Steppe polecat *Mustela eversmanni* (evers-mahn-ee).

In 1758, Carolus Linnaeus, the botanist, wrote the system of classification of plants and animals (taxonomy). He named the domesticated ferret *Mustela furo* (fyoo-roh). The Latin name is said to be based on the ferret's small structure, long, pointed shape and musky odor.

Scientifically, the domesticated ferret is referred to as *Mustela putorius furo*. Putorius is derived from the Latin *putor*, which means *a stench*. This pertains to the ferret's musky odor.

The word ferret is derived from the Latin *furittus*, equivalent to *fur thief*. Ferret also is used as a verb, and according to Webster's Dictionary, it means *to hunt, search about, drive out of hiding place*. These definitions perfectly describe the inherent behavior of our domesticated pet.

☞ **NOTE** Do not assume the pet ferret has the same disposition as its wild cousins. This domesticated mustelid is a gentle, fun-loving animal. The temperament of any domesticated animal is a factor of genetics, environment and treatment.

Some states would have you believe pet ferrets should be classified as wild. However, they have been domesticated for many centuries. It is important to know that in the United States and Canada the ferret is thoroughly domesticated. The pet ferret has no inherent fear of humans and cannot survive without human aid.

Domestication

Before the introduction of the common household cat, farmers relied on the predatory finesse of the polecat to control infestations of rodents and rabbits. The polecat's intelligence, hunting prowess, eloquence and proud play of wild abandon captivated the heart of man.

Polecats selectively were bred based on their ability to be tamed. Through thousands of generations of domestication, the *Mustela putorius* evolved.

The polecat and the domesticated ferret may be genetic kissing cousins, nevertheless, several differences in behavior and physique distinguish these Mustelidae family members.

A SIBERIAN STEPPE POLECAT NAMED PRECIOUS

A DOMESTICATED FERRET NAMED FLAT

Physically the polecat is more muscular and stronger. The ferret, however, generally is slightly larger in size than the polecat, but polecats mature more quickly. At 3 weeks of age, they look like miniature adult polecats, and are already standing up on their hind legs. The polecat has larger ears and teeth, which also are sharper and stronger than the ferret's.

Watching the boundless energy of these kindred spirits is always an adventure, but the polecat, whose legs are longer, is a bit more agile and can climb headfirst or backwards. The polecat also can jump higher and is much faster than its cousin in running.

Polecats have a high level of concentration compared to the short attention span of our domesticated ferret.

Polecats can entertain humans with a faster, more frenzied war dance (a virtual country hoe-down complete with yelping and screeching). But it is the ferret that will prove the friendlier of the two. A polecat would rather hide than be in the company of a stranger, while the domesticated ferret usually will make a beeline to meet a new person.

The ferret's history is as elusive and fleeting - but equally just as interesting - as our free-spirited pet. It enjoys a royal association - from Queen Victoria of England to Genghis Khan of China - but has endured a sometimes difficult transition from its tedious role as a rodent controller to its increasingly popular vocation as a lovable pet.

Ancient literature captures the appearance of the domesticated ferret in the writings of the Greek playwright Aristophanes whose play "Acharnians" was produced in 425 B.C. The term, a "pair of ferrets," pops up in the comedy, demonstrating the existence of the domesticated ferret as well as its talent for stealing. The Egyptians also apparently employed the ferret to rid their granaries of mice. Other occasional ferret references appear in the writings of Aristotle and Strabo.

During the first century, the Roman historian Pliny the Elder described how ferrets were used to hunt rabbits. It is the ferret's innate ability to control rodents and hunt rabbits that made its domestication popular in Augustus Caesar's Roman Empire and into the Middle Ages in Europe and Asia. It is believed Genghis Khan used ferrets for rabbit hunting in 1221 in Afghanistan.

In Europe the ferret became so widely used as a rabbit hunter that a British law in 1319 restricted ownership of ferrets to the nobility. By 1875, Queen Victoria was keeping white-furred, pink-eyed albino ferrets in her castle and offered them as gifts to visiting royalty.

Exactly when ferrets came to North America is not precisely known. Some trace the animal's arrival to 1775, others to 1690 when ferrets were used to catch mice on British ships bringing settlers to New England. As was the case elsewhere, ferrets helped control rodents in the United States. Thousands of ferrets were raised and sold by ferretries until the 1940s when chemical rodenticides were introduced.

With the appearance of underground telephone wiring, ferrets often were used to pull wires through pipes and tight places where human hands could not reach. Their usefulness as "hunters" continues, especially outside North America.

Ferrets, not ones to forget the hospitality of British royalty, returned a kindness when they brought TV cables through the myriads of nooks and crannies underneath St. Paul's Cathedral, thus enabling the world to view the lavish wedding of Prince Charles and Princess Diana.

In North America, ferrets have become increasingly popular as house-hold pets and also are used in biomedical research. There are an estimated 7 million domesticated ferrets in North American house-holds in 1996. THESE COMPANION ANIMALS ARE HERE TO STAY! LET'S LEARN HOW TO TAKE CARE OF THEM PROPERLY.

Description

Ferrets are small, quiet, fastidious and incredibly social. Best of all, you can raise them as comfortably in a one-room apartment as in a house.

The average life span of a ferret bred in North America is 5-7 years. A few live to be 10 and occasionally even older.

Baby ferrets are called KITS. They reach adult weight around 4-6 months and will reach maximum body size (i.e., skeleton size) at 6 months. Females are called JILLS but when spayed are called SPRITES. Males are called HOBS but when neutered are called GIBS. The adult female usually weighs from 3/4 - 2 pounds. The adult male usually weighs a little more, from 2 - 3 1/2 pounds. Like other mustelids, ferrets have beautiful fur coats whose basic color categories are ALBINO and SABLE.

Albino ferrets are pure white with pink eyes. (See photo, p. 25.) Sable ferrets have black legs and tails, with a combination of white or yellow underfur and dark brown or black guard hairs. The distinctive dark mask around their eyes is their trademark. (See photo, p. 17.)

There are other coat colors, which include siamese, butterscotch, cinnamon, black sable, chocolate, silver mitt and panda.

Be aware that ferrets often gain weight during autumn and will lose weight during spring. In addition, hair thickness and length may change. They will have a thick winter coat and less dense summer coat. Mask conformation (distinguishing markings and colors) also may change with season and age.

Ferrets also are known for their musky odor, which is caused by scent and oil glands in the skin. If your ferret has been spayed or neutered, the musky smell virtually is gone because of the decrease in hormones (estrogen or testosterone).

Ferrets, like all carnivores, have anal sacs filled with a strong-smelling secretion with a distinctive odor. The sacs are located on each side of the anus and are the ferret's defense mechanism. The only time a ferret will release this secretion is when it is extremely excited, frightened, angry or feels threatened. The odor dissipates quickly. Ferrets cannot aim this spray.

☞ **NOTE** Removal of the anal sacs (descenting) is not necessary unless there is evidence of a health problem.

Ferrets do have some physical limitations, but they more than make up for them in other areas. While their eyesight and color vision are limited and attention span short, their sense of smell and touch is excellent, and they have wonderful hearing. Their long, slender, agile bodies enable them to elongate their backs, slip into holes and under things in the blink of an eye! Their legs are short and muscular, which allow them to run very quickly through small holes and pipes. Each paw has 5 toes with sharp, nonretractable claws that have excellent grasping ability.

Predatory Behavior

Ferrets, like cats and dogs, are carnivorous animals; they are born hunters. A ferret's predatory behavior affects all aspects of its life. Instinctively, every movement made by the domesticated ferret functions in some way to imitate the actions of its wild ancestors and cousins.

Examples:

♦ When ferrets (especially kits) are roughhousing with each other, they are playing to establish themselves in a dominant role. Play-fighting prepares wild polecat kits for the adult world of carnivores. Play sharpens their instincts and survival skills.

- When ferrets are chuckling and dancing about the room, they are expressing their joy (the Weasel War Dance or Dance of Joy). Wild polecats and other mustelids, such as the weasel or stoat, often will do a dance of joy to celebrate finding a mate or, perhaps, catching prey.

- When ferrets take socks and other items of clothing and store them under couches, dressers or other den-like environments, they are simulating building a nest in an already burrowed hole.

- When ferrets bat a toy around with their paws, then carry it off to a den-like environment, they are playing the part of a predator. Wild polecats hunt, catch prey, kill it, then often carry it to a den-like environment to eat, store it for future use, or, in the case of a female, feed it to her kits.

- In the wild, life is based on necessity. Polecats hunt from dusk to dawn. The well-fed domesticated ferret sleeps through the night. Ferrets adapt their schedule to suit their human parents' way of life. It is a common misconception that domesticated ferrets are nocturnal.

- When ferrets stash uneaten particles of food, they are hoarding surplus food for future use.

All animal behavior can be explained given sufficient patience and ingenuity. Ferrets and other domesticated animals all act instinctively. They all, in some way, try to improve their chances of survival.

Communication

Ferrets communicate through sounds, body language and tenacity.

Excitement

When a ferret is wandering around looking for something, it sometimes will use a low-pitched, mumbling sound. When it finds what it is looking for, there will be a noticeable increase in tonality to signal excitement. When a ferret is excited, it may swish its tail back and forth.

Joy

Ferrets drawn by the desire to express joy often will dance about with or without an audience in sight. Ferrets leap about the room in a spirited style, twisting and chuckling in midair.

Tenacity

Ferrets are persistent. A ferret's goal in life is to get what it wants. For instance, if a ferret wants out of its cage at a particular time, and if not given its way, it may throw a temper tantrum such as digging all the food out of its food bowl, tipping over its water or pooping outside its litter box.

Bored or Tired

A ferret often will flop down, flatten itself out on the floor and stare up at you.

Fear

A frightened ferret will either hunch its back, open its mouth, hiss, bark (a ferret's warning to stay away), screech (a sound that alarms other ferrets in the area), scream, or "bottle-brush" its tail. If not descented, it may release a strong-smelling substance from its anal sacs. Or, as some domesticated ferrets often do, it may simply run and hide. Do not attempt to pick up a frightened ferret, you may get bitten. Some ferrets actually will cry. I knew a ferret who cried every time she got a bath.

Play Behavior

Ferrets are extremely sociable and love both human and animal companionship. Their general outlook is friendly and they accept affectionate handling. Ferrets indulge in a variety of play actions and often do so for hours each day. There are 3 main types of play:

BALL, WHICH HE USES TO RUN HIS FERRET MILE.

NEWFY PLAYING WITH A SMALL, HARD RUBBER

NEWFY LIKES TO PLAY WITH FISHING-POLE-TYPE TOYS

SUCH AS THIS MOUSE ON A STRING.

NEWFY PERFORMING THE WEASEL WAR DANCE.

Social Play

Ferrets often test the limits of their human companions, fellow ferrets, cats and dogs. They engage in teasing, which may include nipping, chasing, roughhousing, and then fleeing from their taunted companions. The roughhousing is fun for ferrets with other ferrets but with cats and dogs it can turn deadly for the ferret if not supervised.

Investigative Play

Ferrets cannot resist the temptation to explore everything. They are famous for investigating, searching, poking and examining anything and everything they can find. Ferrets enjoy adventures in closets, clothes hampers and shoes.

Often, oblivious to danger, daring ferrets will squeeze their way through any hole wider than 1 inch in diameter or escape through an open door to discover a world of unfamiliar giants, noises and smells. Ferrets need to be protected from the hazards of their play behavior.

In comparison, the ferret's wild cousins explore new territory that offers food and shelter. Wild animals usually know the pitfalls and dangers, except, of course, when it involves humans.

Acrobatic Play

Ferrets, like kittens and puppies, spend their childhood exploring their physical capabilities. Ferrets leap, jump, twist, roll, run and even somersault, expending a great amount of energy during this testing time. But, unlike cats and dogs, ferrets will spend a lifetime taking risks.

The Mind Of The Ferret

FERRETS ARE INTELLIGENT LITTLE CRITTERS. Given the right motivation, they have an uncanny ability to solve any problem. Never underestimate them! For example, if you close the door to a forbidden room, your ferret probably will be sitting outside trying to invent a way to get in.

If you happen to be in that room, your ferret most likely will be sitting outside just waiting for you to open the door to outmaneuver you and dash into the room. For ferrets, an off-limits area is a challenge to be conquered. Perhaps the ferret motto should be: "WHERE THERE'S A WAY, THERE'S A WILL!"

Ferrets learn good and bad habits from each other. My Newfy taught Twiggy to dip her head in her water bowl, swoosh the water around and shake it all over the place. This was cute but together they go the extra mile. They do not stop until every drop of water is gone.

They also love to steal and hide things where only they can find them. Twiggy gets into my dresser drawers and steals all my socks. Newfy takes my gym shoes and steals the cat's toys. They BOTH steal my keys!

The Merry "Little Thief"

Chapter 2
CHOOSING A FERRET

Why a Ferret?

Is owning a pet ferret a well-thought-out decision or a spur-of-the-moment impulse?

Can you afford the cost of ferret ownership: veterinary care, housing essentials such as a cage, food, litter, bedding, dishes?

Have you given a pet away or dropped it off at a shelter because you were moving or the pet became too much trouble? Pets bond quickly and never will understand being abandoned.

Do you have an infant or young child? Strict supervision is recommended at all times.

Have you consulted your family and considered the needs of the animals you already have?

Is this pet a "surprise gift"? Please allow the owner to select the right pet in person.

Does your landlord allow pets? Only certain pets? Are there too many pets in the household already? Do you own dogs originally bred for hunting? Do you own birds, rabbits, mice or reptiles?

Did you know that ferrets are high-maintenance pets? The primary caretaker must be a responsible adult.

Are Ferrets Legal In The Area Or State In Which You Live?

☞ **WARNING** As of March 1996 ferrets still are illegal in California and Hawaii. There also are a variety of restrictions within counties or cities in other states. For this reason, check BEFORE you acquire a ferret because it could be confiscated and put to death.

A lack of education regarding the domesticated ferret has generated the following voiced concerns.

Concern Ferrets are wild animals.

Fact Ferrets are domesticated. (See What Is A Ferret?, p. 15 and Food For Thought, p. 35.)

Concern Ferrets will produce feral (untamed) populations if they escape from their homes or are released in the wild.

Fact There are no known feral populations of the domesticated ferret in North America. Our pet ferret cannot exist without human aid. (See NOTE, p. 16.) Additionally, the majority of pet ferrets are spayed or neutered before being sold.

Concern Ferrets are a risk to children and should be banned.

Fact All animals are a potential risk to children. (See Understanding Animal Behavior, p. 74 and WARNING and NOTE, p. 77.)

Concern Ferrets are a threat to agriculture and wildlife.

Fact The domesticated ferret is legal in 48 states. Studies conducted by the California Domestic Ferret Association have shown that this pet has had no impact on wildlife or agricultural interests (crops and livestock).

For further information about the ferret's legal status in your area, contact a ferret shelter or organization near you. (See Chapter 12.)

Where To Get Your Ferret & What To Look For

In your quest to add a ferret to your family, you will find that you have a pretty good selection of sources: pet stores, ferret shelters, breeders, newspapers or friends. The initial process is basically the same as getting any new pet. You will want to find one that is happy, healthy, friendly, and, of course, just right for you.

Certain criteria should be met in choosing a ferret, no matter where you get your new companion.

HERE ARE SOME VERY SPECIFIC THINGS TO LOOK FOR:

Health
The ferret should be alert and active with bright eyes and a full, soft, shiny fur coat.

Disposition
Look for a curious, gentle nature. Be aware that baby ferrets, like kittens and puppies, frequently nip. However, they will outgrow this stage. If you find one that bites and hangs on, I would recommend hands off. You may have problems. Color or sex is meaningless in terms of disposition.

☞ NOTE Spayed Or Neutered Ferrets
It is imperative that your ferrets be spayed or neutered. It will guarantee that ferret overpopulation does not become a problem as it has with cats and dogs. It also helps avoid undesirable behavior and some medical problems. (See Sterilization, p. 41.) Many pet shop ferrets already have been altered and descented by commercial breeders. Ask for proof.

The Kits

THE PET STORE

Pet stores usually are the first choice for most first-time pet buyers. Consequently, pet stores have an obligation to be fully informed about the ferret's unique needs. Pet stores also have the initial responsibility to provide you, the consumer, with accurate information about the ferret's background. Employees should have thorough knowledge of what products are essential to the health and welfare of the domesticated ferret.

Many pet ferrets in North America are abused, abandoned, placed in shelters or are unjustly euthanized because their needs are not understood.

THE FERRET SHELTER

Ferret shelters have ferrets of all ages. Do not assume your new pet has to be a baby. Ferrets of any age make great pets and older ones are not quite as rambunctious as babies. They are a little easier to handle if you are a first-time ferret owner. My first little one, Wheezee, was 6 months old when I got her. My second ferret, Pepper, was 4 years old. Twiggy was 8 months old and Newfy was 6 months old.

Ferret shelters most likely will have prescreened the ferret for temperament and any available history will be provided.

Advantages Of Adopting An Older Ferret

I adopted Pepper Head to keep my 3-year-old Wheezee Girl company. Together they were mature (no more terrible twos), about the same energy level, great company for one another and wonderful companions for me. Pepper was such a gentle-natured ferret and never nipped, destroyed anything, learned any new bad habits or threw any temper tantrums. I had him only 2 1/2 years. But in that short time he gave both Wheezee and me a steady supply of sunshine.

The Shelter Ferret

☞ **NOTE** Ferret shelters do need help in taking care of the hundreds of lost, found, unwanted, unadoptable, ill and aging ferrets. You can help by adopting or fostering a ferret, or, donating money for medical costs and supplies. Donations of old T-shirts and sweat shirts may be used as bedding, and old towels for use in bathing the ferrets. Your contributions will be gratefully appreciated ♥...

BREEDERS

You also can get your ferret directly from a breeder. Call a shelter or a ferret organization for the names of responsible breeders.

NEWSPAPER, FRIENDS OR NEIGHBORS

If you buy your ferret through a newspaper ad or obtain a ferret from a friend or neighbor, you will want to find out as much as you can about the animal's health, medical and family history, age and diet.

Ask if the ferret had been caged. If it was not and was allowed to have free run of the home, it is going to have an adjustment adapting to a cage for safekeeping.

This is important information to have because it normally takes at least 2 weeks for a ferret to adapt to a new home. That includes new people, sights, smells, a new place to sleep, maybe even a new diet, not to mention other ferrets and household pets.

If You Find A Ferret

It is completely within the realm of possibility to find a stray ferret. If you decide you want to keep it, check with your neighbors, the local Humane Society and the local ferret shelter first. Make sure the animal is not someone's pet that has escaped or was reported lost. If it isn't, immediately make an appointment with a veterinarian for a checkup.

Obviously, if you find a ferret, you are not going to have any idea of its background, but its temperament should be evident in very little time.

Your veterinarian should be able to tell you the approximate age and any medical problems that are present.

A slow increase in human interaction may be necessary before a ferret will once more become outgoing and friendly. Be patient. Remember, adapting takes time.

If you find a ferret and do not want to keep it, call the local ferret shelter. Remember, domesticated ferrets are NOT wild animals and must NEVER be turned loose! They simply cannot survive outside and may die from exposure, predators or starvation within a few days ☹.

☞ **A WORD OF WARNING** If you find a ferret, approach it with caution. The little critter probably has been through a rough time, which may include malnutrition, dehydration and exposure to weather and predators. It may bite out of fear. Although it is extremely remote, a stray ferret could have contracted rabies from an infected animal. Therefore, the ferret should be handled with great care and turned over to a ferret shelter or taken to a veterinarian for a thorough checkup. The ferret may need to be quarantined, depending on the guidelines of your state or locality.

The Unwanted Ferret

First and foremost, one has a moral duty to protect an innocent life. By law, the safety and well-being of a ferret (or any pet) must never be jeopardized. Do not abandon your pet!

Abandoned animals live a life of fear. Left unsupported they are tormented by hunger, thirst, disease, weather extremes, preying wildlife, other discarded pets, the cruel acts of some children and adults, and motorized vehicles. Their suffering often ends in a painful death.

Be loyal to your pet. Call a ferret shelter or find a caring home for your unwanted pet.

A SPECIAL REQUEST

PLEASE DO NOT BREED YOUR PET FERRET. THERE ARE THOUSANDS OF UNWANTED FERRETS IN SHELTERS THAT NEED CARING HOMES. WE DO NOT NEED A TRAGIC OVERPOPULATION OF FERRETS.

In an ASPCA (The American Society for the Prevention of Cruelty to Animals) newsletter, Roger A. Caras, president, writes that "one unspayed female dog and her descendants can produce 4,372 puppies in just 7 generations. One unspayed cat and her offspring can produce 80 million kittens in 10 years."

Millions of unwanted and stray dogs and cats are euthanized by animal shelters every year. Millions die tragically on the streets.

If everyone would take the time to have a stray domesticated animal spayed or neutered that would help end the overpopulation and put an end to needless pain, fear and suffering.

Make a commitment to have your pet spayed or neutered.

FOOD FOR THOUGHT

In the wild, animals are taught quickly by their mothers how to survive on their own. Inherently, wild animals know that whatever is dangerous must be avoided. Once fully weaned they take care of their own needs.

All household pets originated from a wild species. Now that man has made domesticated animals dependent upon us, their needs must be met by us. Domesticated animals cannot take care of their own needs.

Just like children, animals must first be loved before they can learn to trust, feel safe and free to explore their natural sense of curiosity; to rejoice in life for life itself and live in the moment, to be the very wonders that they are.

A pet is a privilege and a lifetime of responsibility.

Chapter 3
YOUR FERRET'S FIRST CHECKUP

Tommy & His Veterinarian

The Initial Examination

This checkup is vital to your pet's long-term health. YOU SHOULD TAKE YOUR NEW FERRET TO A VETERINARIAN (one who has experience in ferret medicine) FOR ITS FIRST CHECKUP AND SHOTS WITHIN 24 TO 48 HOURS OF PURCHASE.

Arrive at the veterinary clinic with your ferret safely locked inside a travel carrier equipped with a water bottle. Remember, as clean as all veterinarians try to keep their clinics, sick animals come and go, so keep your pet to yourself and off the floor.

The initial examination should include the following:

♦ A PHYSICAL

A physical examination should include a thorough investigation of the entire ferret's body, including the eyes, ears and mouth. A stethoscope is used to listen to the heart and lungs. The abdomen should be thoroughly palpated. If recommended, a fecal exam should be performed for intestinal parasites. Bring a fresh stool sample (in a small plastic bag or container) from each of your ferrets.

♦ BLOOD TESTS (if recommended)

♦ HEARTWORM PREVENTION

Heartworm is a parasite that is transmitted to your pet by a mosquito bite. Heartworm preventative is given monthly and is a must because heartworm disease can be fatal!

Even if your pet does not go outdoors, mosquitoes do come inside. It only takes 1 infected mosquito to inject heartworm larvae into a ferret's bloodstream. The larvae develop into adult worms (5"-6" long) eventually lodging in the heart, leading to the ferret's death.

HEARTWORM DISEASE WARNING SIGNS

♦ Chronic cough ♦ Lethargy ♦ Labored breathing ♦ Fluid accumulation in the abdomen ♦ Fainting ♦ Bluish color to tongue, gums and lips ♦

♦ VACCINATIONS AGAINST CANINE DISTEMPER

Kits If a pet store or breeder tells you that a ferret has had its canine distemper shot, this only refers to the initial distemper vaccination, which was given at approximately 6 weeks of age. YOUR FERRET STILL WILL REQUIRE ADDITIONAL VACCINATIONS AT 2-3 WEEK INTERVALS UNTIL THE SERIES IS COMPLETE AT 14 WEEKS OF AGE. Annual boosters will provide continuous protection.

Adult Ferrets (14 weeks of age and older) If previously unvaccinated, ferrets will require 2 vaccinations 2-3 weeks apart. Annual boosters will provide continuous protection.

Canine distemper is a virus that is shed from an infected animal through sneezing, coughing, eye discharge, urine, feces and skin debris. THIS DISEASE CAN BE SPREAD AMONG ANIMALS THROUGH DIRECT CONTACT, IT CAN BE CARRIED ON HUMAN CLOTHING AND SKIN FOR AT LEAST 8 HOURS OR IT CAN TRAVEL THROUGH THE AIR. THIS VIRUS ALSO CAN LIVE IN THE ENVIRONMENT FOR WEEKS.

CANINE DISTEMPER VIRTUALLY IS 100% FATAL IN INFECTED FERRETS! The only protection is vaccination. The Department of Agriculture licensed the first canine distemper virus (CDV) vaccine for use in ferrets in 1992 (Fervac-D, United Vaccines, Madison, WI). Your pet will be at risk of contracting this disease if the series of vaccinations is not completed.

CANINE DISTEMPER WARNING SIGNS

♦ Loss of appetite ♦ Thick, yellow or green, sticky eye discharge ♦ Swollen eyelids ♦ Green or yellow nasal discharge ♦ Swelling of the lips, chin and anus ♦ Thick brown crusts that form on the eyes, nose, lips, chin and anus ♦ Lethargy ♦ Diarrhea ♦ Thickening and hardening of the paw pads ♦ Orange crusting of the skin in the abdominal and anal areas ♦ Muscle tremors, hyper-excitability and convulsions ♦

♦ VACCINATION AGAINST RABIES

A rabies vaccine can be given safely at the age of 3 months (no earlier), then boostered annually.

Rabies is an incurable viral disease. This virus attacks the central nervous system of warm-blooded animals, including humans. With rare exceptions, rabies is fatal. The virus, which is present in the salivary glands of infected animals, usually is transmitted through a bite or a break in the skin.

The United States Department of Agriculture licensed a rabies vaccine for use in domesticated ferrets in 1990 (Imrab-R, Rhone-Merieux, Athens, GA).

Ask your veterinarian for a certificate of vaccination, which should include the following:

♦ The name and lot number of the vaccination used

♦ The date it was administered and length of effectiveness

♦ To whom it was given: age, sex, species, color and name

☞ **NOTE** It is wise to vaccinate your ferret against rabies because...

♦ It may escape from your home and be bitten by an infected animal.

♦ Young children may sometimes provoke a ferret to bite.

♦ People who are unfamiliar or afraid of ferrets may mishandle your pet, which could create a bite situation.

♦ When you travel, vaccination certificates are required.

♦ Ferrets that are boarded or temporarily housed outside are at risk of other animals.

☞ **WARNING** The shedding period (the exact amount of time it takes for ferrets to shed the rabies virus in their saliva prior to the development of clinical signs) of the rabies virus in ferrets has not been established.

In the event that a ferret bite is reported to local health authorities, the ferret most likely will be confiscated, euthanized, its head removed, then its brain tissue examined for rabies by a qualified laboratory designated by the local or state health department. In some areas of the country, bite situations are evaluated on a case-by-case basis. Sometimes the ferret's life is spared if the ferret has been vaccinated against rabies. Do you know the policy of your local health department?

Protect the life of your ferret. Do not allow strangers to touch your pet. Do not allow friends, relatives or children to handle your pet without strict supervision. Do not allow your ferret to be exposed to wildlife and other stray animals.

GOOD NEWS

Research to establish the rabies shedding period in the ferret currently is being conducted at the Centers for Disease Control in Atlanta, Georgia, under the direction of Dr. Charles Rupprecht. It is believed that an adequate isolation and quarantine time can be established in ferrets.

☞ **NOTE** Dr. Deborah J. Briggs, director of the Rabies Lab at Kansas State University, is helping to coordinate the shedding study. Anyone wishing to donate money to the research project may send a tax-deductible donation to :

Kansas State University Foundation
C/O Dr. Deborah J. Briggs
College of Veterinary Medicine
Manhattan, KS 66502
Attn.: Rabies in Ferrets Project

Always keep your ferret up to date on its vaccinations. (See Preventive Veterinary Care, p. 124.) Ask for a health record booklet so you can keep track of your ferret's medical history.

VACCINATION PRECAUTIONS

Some ferrets may have allergic reactions to the distemper or rabies vaccines. This reaction, known as anaphylaxis, occurs when a ferret becomes hypersensitive to one or more components of the vaccine.

Within 15 minutes of being vaccinated, a ferret experiencing anaphylaxis may exhibit one or more of the following signs: pain at the injection site, lethargy, vomiting, diarrhea (with or without blood) or collapse.

If an allergic reaction occurs, the veterinarian will administer medications to counteract the reaction, reduce inflammation and improve circulation. Fluids may be given intravenously (into the veins) or subcutaneously (beneath the skin) to combat shock.

To be on the safe side, please remain with your ferret at the veterinarian's office for at least 30 minutes after your pet has been vaccinated.

IF YOUR FERRET HAS A REACTION TO A VACCINE AFTER YOU HAVE LEFT THE VETERINARIAN'S OFFICE, RETURN IMMEDIATELY. If the ferret has gone into shock, keep it warm but not hot.

Most veterinarians recommend that ferrets with previous reactions to a vaccine be premedicated an hour before the vaccination with an antihistamine injection. This can prevent an allergic reaction. Keep the ferret at the office for 30 minutes after the vaccination.

DO NOT VACCINATE A PET THAT IS EXHIBITING SIGNS OF ILLNESS.

Sterilization

The natural breeding cycle of the domesticated ferret is determined by the length of daylight and environmental temperature. In the Northern Hemisphere, March through August is the general breeding season. In the Southern Hemisphere, it is September through February. Because daylight is the governing factor, ferret breeders frequently will control the breeding cycles with artificial light. Under natural light conditions, females can have 2 litters a year.

Ferrets reach sexual maturity at 4-8 months of age. If the babies are born in the fall and are under natural lighting, they will not reach sexual maturity until the following spring. If they are born in the spring, they will reach sexual maturity during the summer. Many ferrets are now spayed and neutered at 4-6 weeks of age and never reach sexual maturity.

Ferrets are capable of breeding within the year they are born. In view of this fact, it is recommended that jills (female ferrets) be spayed (removal of both the ovaries and uterus) and hobs (male ferrets) be neutered (removal of both testicles).

Signs Of A Male In Season

◆ A strong, musky odor (from skin oils and urine)

◆ A deep, golden-yellow undercoat (staining from skin oils)

◆ The male will mark its territory with urine, and during breeding season groom himself with his urine. The male's lower abdomen will be wet due to constant urine dribbling.

◆ The male may become aggressive.

◆ There may be significant amounts of weight loss.

Signs Of A Female In Estrus (Heat)

◆ Swollen vulva (See photo, p. 129) with a pink, watery secretion. Dampness from the watery discharge may allow bacteria to reproduce near the opening to the bladder. Bladder infections are possible.

◆ Prolonged heat periods can cause hair loss. The hair thins at the base of the tail, inside of the legs then gradually over most of the body. Hair will grow back once the ferret is spayed or out of heat.

◆ Prolonged heat periods also can result in aplastic anemia (severe suppression of the bone marrow): pale gums, nose, ears and paw pads.

◆ An unspayed female may have a personality change along with a strong, musky body odor. The female may urinate more frequently (leaving the scent for the male), and continually be wet around the vulva and back of the thighs. The urine will have a strong odor due to an increase in sex hormones.

◆ Aggressive nipping behavior

UNSPAYED FEMALES

When an unspayed female goes into estrus, the ovaries produce estrogen, preparing the uterus for implantation and pregnancy. A female ferret most likely will remain in heat until she is bred or artificially brought out of estrus with a hormone shot from the veterinarian. (Some ferrets do not respond to hormone shots.)

If a ferret is not taken out of estrus, she eventually may develop aplastic anemia. This condition develops during the long estrus period when high levels of estrogen circulate in the blood. Over a period of one month or longer the high estrogen levels can suppress production of red and white blood cells and platelets in the bone marrow. Decreased production of these cells renders the ferret more susceptible to infection and injuries, and in addition, the blood cannot clot. Eventually, this condition becomes irreversible and **the ferret dies.**

The signs of aplastic anemia often are not apparent until the ferret is seriously, sometimes critically ill. THEREFORE, IF YOU HAVE AN UN-SPAYED FEMALE, YOU ABSOLUTELY MUST NOT ALLOW HER TO STAY IN ESTRUS IF YOU ARE NOT GOING TO BREED HER! TAKE HER TO THE VETERINARIAN AS SOON AS POSSIBLE.

☛ **WARNING** An unspayed female (jill) can be spayed while in heat and should be spayed within 4 weeks of the first signs of estrus. The longer the heat period, the greater the risk of aplastic anemia.

☞ **NOTE** If a female ferret is spayed incompletely (all ovarian tissue is not removed) or has adrenal gland disease (See pp. 127 & 129), she may show signs of estrus. Exploratory surgery may be necessary to determine the problem.

A NEW FERRET OWNER SHOULD LOCATE A VETERINARY EMERGENCY CLINIC WITH EXPERIENCE IN FERRET MEDICINE BEFORE AN EMERGENCY OCCURS.

Chapter 4
SHOPPING & SAFETY GUIDELINES

Tommy & Twinkle Go Shopping

Before You Shop

Do your homework! Read through this entire book, it will tell you what kind of products are essential to the health and welfare of your ferret. Make a list.

You should walk into a pet store armed with knowledge. If you don't, sales people who are not ferret care experts may sell you products that are completely unsafe, unsuitable or both for your ferret.

I recommend that you ask questions and fully understand the products that may be offered by pet stores, catalogs, ferret shelters, veterinarians or breeders.

A Suitable Cage (Do's & Don'ts)

When you bring your ferret home, WHERE in your home is your ferret going to live? Unlike cats or dogs, ferrets simply cannot be given free run; it is too dangerous. A suitable cage is an absolute must! (See photo, p. 49)

I usually advise people NOT to bring their ferret home from the place of purchase unless they bring a cage. There are some DO's and DON'Ts on cages. If you follow them in the beginning, you will save money, time, and heartache in the long run.

DO's

- 👍 Do buy a sturdy wire cage.

- 👍 Do get a big enough cage. At least 30"-36" long, 16"-18" wide, and a minimum of 18" high. Some rabbit cages are suitable as ferret cages. THE BIGGER THE CAGE, THE BETTER!

- 👍 Do buy a cage with plenty of floor space. Ferrets are not happy in cages with steep ramps and small ledges. Ferrets are ground-dwelling animals that like to go into underground burrows and tunnels to sleep. They are not tree climbers like cats.

- 👍 Do make sure the cage door has an opening big enough for a litter box to fit through.

- 👍 Do make sure the cage is escape-proof with a strong latch. If it is not, your ferret will try to squeeze through any open space. If it tries to get out that way and gets stuck, the results could be fatal. Be careful with spring latches.

- 👍 Do use a washable piece of carpet, or something just as soft, for the cage floor. Ferret paws were not designed for wire floors.

☝ Do make sure the cage has a distinct sleeping, feeding and toilet area. (See Ferret Necessities, p. 48.) The litter pan should be kept at a distance from the sleeping and eating area. It is a good idea to secure the litter pan to one corner of the cage.

☝ Do keep the cage in a cool, shaded, dry area away from drafts and direct sunlight. Ferrets have a limited number of sweat glands and are most comfortable in temperatures 65°-75° F. They cannot tolerate temperatures above 80°F (27°C) or high humidity. If your ferret becomes overheated, it could die of heatstroke within minutes. (See Heatstroke, p. 141.) REMEMBER that humidity and direct sunlight greatly will affect the temperature. In warm weather, ferrets drink more water.

☝ Do take your ferret out of its cage. Give your pet at least 1 hour (more is better) of exercise on a daily basis and include lots of love and companionship.

☝ Do keep the cage clean. Use a nontoxic disinfectant in HOT water to help destroy germs.

☝ Do put your ferret in its cage when it is tired. Also, cage your pet when you are not at home; during parties; when guests or strangers are coming and going, or during any other unique or unfamiliar occasion you can think of to prevent tragic accidents.

☝ Do make sure aging ferrets easily can get in and out of their cages. Use ramps if necessary. Aging ferrets may become weak in the hind legs for a variety of reasons.

☞ **SPECIAL NOTE** The domesticated ferret is an indoor pet. If it must be temporarily housed outside, the cage must be sheltered from wind, rain, snow, sun, heat and cold. Do not house ferrets below 55° F. Ferrets must always have a nest-like environment to stay warm. (See Bedding, p. 51.)

If you cannot find the cage you need at the pet store, call a shelter or a ferret organization near you. (See Chapter 12.) They usually can tell you where to purchase a suitable cage.

DON'Ts

☞ Don't purchase small cages as ferret housing. (See photo of Unsuitable Cages, p. 49.)

☞ Don't purchase cages with small ledges and steep ramps. Ferrets are burrowing animals that require plenty of floor space in their cages.

☞ Don't use painted or pressure-treated woods or metals containing toxins such as zinc or lead as housing material.

☞ Don't use an aquarium as a cage. Aquariums are unsanitary and unhealthy places to keep ferrets. The ventilation is terrible. The damp (caused by ferret's urine) and stale air causes respiratory problems. AQUARIUMS ARE FOR FISH, NOT FERRETS.

☞ Don't use cedar or pine chips in ferret cages. (See WARNING, p. 52.)

☞ Don't put the cage in direct sunlight, in the draft of an air-conditioning vent, room air-conditioner or where there is dampness such as in some basements.

☞ Don't place the cage next to a TV or stereo. Place the cage in a quiet area.

THE FERRET'S DOMAIN

A cage is like a den for ferrets. Since their ancestors were den animals, it is necessary to provide a private, den-like place for them to sleep.

My "babies" eat, sleep and poop in their ferret "condo" (2-story cage) until they are ready to play. But I always leave the cage door open when they are out because they often go back on their own to sleep, eat and to SOMETIMES use the litter box. And while they like their freedom when they come out to play, they also like the security of their den-like environment.

SLEEP HABITS

You soon will begin to notice that your ferret will sleep 15-20 hours a day. As a matter of fact, a ferret sleeps so soundly and relaxed that at times you might think your ferret has died. Simply put your fingers against its chest and feel for a heartbeat. You also will notice that it will adjust its sleep schedule to suit your schedule. Your little companion will be waiting for you in the morning and at night.

☞ **NOTE** Do not leave your ferret in the cage for an extended period of time. If you do not allow your ferret exercise, love and companionship on a DAILY BASIS, it will gain unnecessary weight, develop stiff joints and muscles, become very stressed, unhappy and may become difficult to handle. In the morning, my ferrets play for 1-2 hours, and at night, they play as long as they want.

Ferret Necessities

You have the cage. Now you have to furnish it, plus provide other items important to your ferret's health and comfort. What should you get? The list below is short, but essential.

FOOD DISH

A ceramic or weighted dish usually cannot be tipped over. Make sure the dishes are not painted with lead-based enamel. Bowls that attach to the side of the cage are an alternative.

WATER BOTTLE

Buy the size made for small animals (16 oz.). Attach it to the outside of the cage with the spout facing in. Your ferret cannot knock it over this way. The sipper tube should be placed at a comfortable drinking level, approximately 6" from the floor of the cage. Clean the water bottle and the stainless steel sipper tube daily with hot, soapy water. Rinse it with clear water. Replace water bottles as needed.

FERRETS REQUIRE
ROOMY CAGES WITH
PLENTY OF FLOOR
SPACE AND THE
NECESSARY
ESSENTIALS
PICTURED HERE.

**A SUITABLE CAGE
APPROVED BY
TWIGGY AND NEWFY**

APPROPRIATE
BEDDING

PLENTY OF
FLOOR SPACE

16 OZ. WATER
BOTTLE

LITTER BOX

WATER BOWL
AND FOOD DISH
ATTACHED TO
CAGE

**UNSUITABLE
FERRET
HOUSING**

TOO SMALL

Squeeze the water bottle daily to make sure water is coming through the sipper tube. Sometimes the tube gets clogged with saliva, leaving the ferret without access to water. For this reason, I also recommend providing the ferret with an additional water bottle or a bowl of water. Make sure the water bowl is weighted. Change the water twice daily. Ferrets enjoy drinking from a water bowl. Always place food and water next to each other in the cage. Ferrets do not eat unless water is readily available.

☞ **NOTE** Some ferrets have difficulty learning to use the water bottle. If you use a water bottle, keep an eye on the water level. Make sure that the ferret is getting plenty of water, which is vital to its well-being.

LITTER PAN & POOP SCOOP

Use a pan with high sides (more than 4") with one side cut down for easy access. Ferrets back into corners, raise their tails, then do their business. A metal or plastic poop scoop works well.

LITTER

Pelleted products made from paper or plant fibers are excellent. These products usually are available at pet stores or specialty shops. If the litter is unavailable, ask to have it ordered for you. Prices will vary.

☞ **NOTE** Scoopable litter is not recommended because it irritates the ferret's eyes and may cause respiratory problems. Clay litter has dust, little odor control and may lead to a dry coat. Corncob litter is not very absorbent, has little odor control and easily grows mold. Cedar and pine chips may cause respiratory problems. (See WARNING, p. 52.)

Although rare, a foreign object such as a litter particle can become lodged in a ferret's nasal passages. If your ferret has persistent sneezing accompanied by nasal discharge, head shaking and pawing at the mouth, take your ferret to the veterinarian.

ODOR NEUTRALIZER

Use nontoxic, nonirritating, odor-eliminating products to clean up ferret mistakes. These products usually are available at your veterinarian's office or at a pet store.

BEDDING

Ferrets must have a nest-like environment to sleep. If you do not provide one, ferrets will choose their own by burrowing inside places such as a couch, a dresser drawer or an appliance.

Ferrets Prefer The Following:

- 👍 100% cotton T-shirts and sweat shirts. Be sure to remove all buttons, zippers and string-like material because ferrets like to chew on them. They could cause intestinal blockage and possible death if swallowed.
- 👍 100% cotton baby blankets
- 👍 Hammocks or special-order sleep sacks

SHOPPING TIPS

Buy bedding that can be washed at least 50 times before falling apart. Change the bedding every 3 days to prevent odors. I advise purchasing additional bedding. DO NOT use perfumed detergents or fabric softeners on their bedding because some ferrets are allergic to the chemicals.

Do Not Use:

- 👎 Worn, shredded T-shirts or towels because a ferret's nails could easily get caught. A nail may be torn out while the ferret struggles to free itself.
- 👎 Sawdust - respiratory risk and irritates eyes
- 👎 Newspaper - The ink will discolor your ferret's coat and paws.
- 👎 Cedar or pine chips - respiratory risk

☞ **WARNING** For years, cedar and pine chips have been used as bedding for many species of small mammals, including ferrets. However, over the past 10 years, increasing evidence is emerging that this is not a good choice.

Cedar and yellow pine shavings, as well as other aromatic, soft woods, release volatile hydrocarbons, which adversely may affect those animals that continually inhale these substances. Plicatic acid, a volatile hydrocarbon found in cedar, has been documented as causing asthma in humans and rabbits. Other volatile hydrocarbons result in changes in the liver of rodents and other small mammals, which may impair the animal's ability to detoxify certain drugs, including anesthetic agents. Cedar shavings also have been incriminated in increased mortality in baby rats.

If you have to use a wood chip, use aspen chips. They are relatively dust- and odor-free.

A TRAVEL CARRIER

A small, well-ventilated carrier equipped with a water bottle is fine for transporting your ferret to and from the veterinarian and on other short trips. A loose ferret in a car is dangerous for you and your pet.

SUITABLE TOYS

Ferrets LOVE having their own toys. The toys should not have small pieces that can be bitten off and swallowed. The acceptable ones include:

- Small, HARD RUBBER balls with a bell inside
- Infant toys such as terry-covered, soft rattles (toys that make noise)
- Clothes dryer vent hose, PVC pipe (available at most hardware stores in various lengths). Blue jeans also make great tunnels through which ferrets love to crawl.

IN →

TUNNELING IS OUR FAVORITE SPORT

OUT ←

- A cardboard box or paper bag will keep your ferrets amused for at least 5 minutes.

- Ferrets have great fun chasing toys that are attached to a string on a stick (resembling a fishing pole).

- "Stolen" ferret treasures such as socks, gloves, shoes and your car keys

TOY WARNINGS

The fishing-pole-type toy with the "floaty" object (feathers, fabric, fluff or tinsel) is fun for ferrets or cats to chase, but do not leave any of these hand-held toys around when you are not supervising the game. Ferrets could chew on and swallow the materials.

If your ferret chews a hole through one of its toys, throw the object away! Ingested toys can cause intestinal blockage and possible death. SOFT LATEX AND RUBBER CAT OR DOG TOYS ARE THE NO. 1 CAUSE OF GASTROINTESTINAL BLOCKAGE.

☞ **NOTE** If you notice your ferret has eaten something that could cause an obstruction, use a cat hairball laxative. It can be used at 1/2 tsp. 2-3 times a day for 1-2 days. *If your ferret is vomiting, do not use a cat hairball laxative.* Immediately take your ferret to the veterinarian. It is important to read Gastrointestinal Disorder Warning Signs, p. 131.

If you see the eaten material protruding out of its anal area, give the ferret 1 hour to pass it on its own. If the ferret exhibits pain when trying to pass the foreign material or if the material does not completely pass, take your pet to the veterinarian. Do not try to remove the material yourself, you may do more damage.

A LOUD, SQUEAKY TOY

This special toy should have a sound distinctive from your ferret's other toys. Some ferrets prefer one sound over another.

Use This Toy Only When...

- ◆ Your ferret is sleeping in a hard-to-reach area and you want it to wake up and come to you.

- ◆ You cannot find your ferret in the house and you want it to come to you. (See Escapes & Captures, p. 66.)

- ◆ Your ferrets are fighting. They usually will stop and come running.

☞ **NOTE** When you squeak the toy and the ferret comes running, give it a reward, A FAVORITE TREAT. This way it will associate the sound of this toy with the treat. Also, use this toy if your ferret escapes from home. Hopefully, the ferret will hear the sound and come running to get its reward.

Because ferrets are intelligent critters, they soon will learn what this sound means. I use a squeaky toy once a day when I am about to leave for work. I go into their room where their cage is and squeak away. Twigg and Newfy come running every day.

The Intelligent Ferret

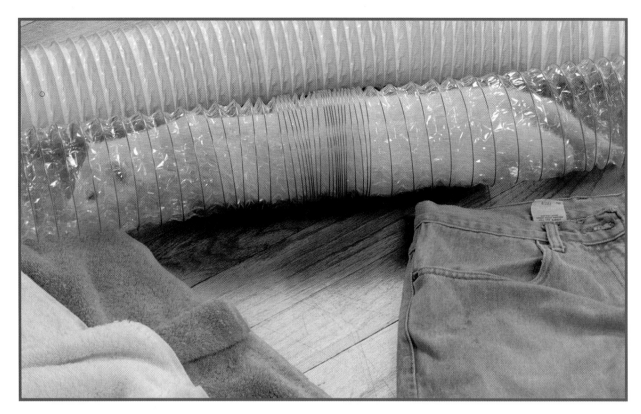

NEWFY INVESTIGATING HIS NEW TUNNEL.

LET'S PLAY!   LET'S PLAY!

THIS
TUNNEL
IS A LITTLE
TOO SMALL
FOR
NEWFY'S
WINTER
FAT.

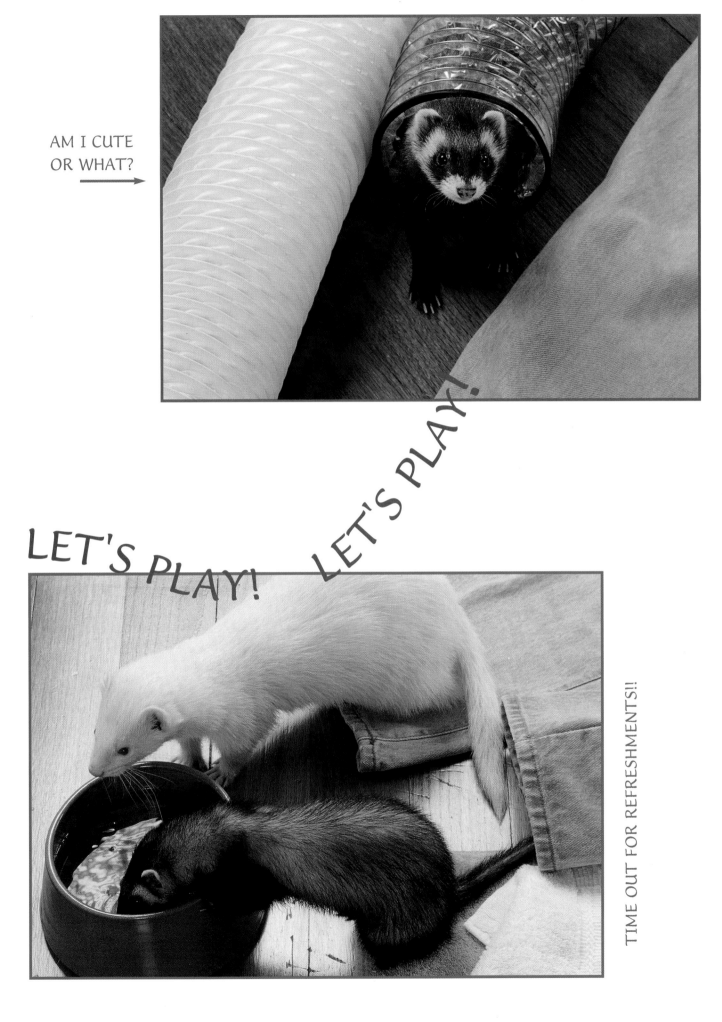

AM I CUTE
OR WHAT?

LET'S PLAY!

LET'S PLAY!   LET'S PLAY!

TIME OUT FOR REFRESHMENTS!!

Tommy Eats A Well-Balanced Diet

Diet

WATER

Ferrets must have access to water at all times, including playtime outside their cage! Change water daily. You might consider using filtered or bottled water. It is healthier for you and your ferret than ordinary tap water.

FOOD

FERRETS ARE NOT VEGETARIANS. FERRETS ARE OBLIGATE CARNIVORES, which means they must have a diet that is HIGH IN ANIMAL PROTEIN (MORE THAN 32%) AND FAT (MORE THAN 18%). The ferret's reliance on animal tissue comes from its evolution as a predator. It has a rapid metabolism and food will pass through its digestive tract in 3-4 hours. Therefore, ferrets need to eat frequently and probably will consume several small meals a day. KEEP THEIR DISHES FILLED AT ALL TIMES! Give them fresh food daily.

☞ **_NOTE_** Kits (baby ferrets) must be fed a diet moistened lightly with water until they have their adult teeth (about 10 weeks of age). Gradually use less and less water until your ferret adjusts to a completely dry diet. Moistened food should be changed twice daily to avoid spoilage.

Premium ferret foods always should be the No. 1 choice. Quality food will have the single greatest impact on the ferret's health and lifelong well-being. If you cannot find premium ferret foods at your local pet store, ask to have one ordered. In the meantime, premium kitten/cat foods are a good substitute. Ferret and kitten foods can be mixed together. Read the ingredients to make certain that there is enough animal protein and fat.

Ultimately, the quality of any food is best measured by how the pet looks, feels and acts. A healthy ferret should have bright eyes, silky hair, supple skin and pass well-formed, small stools without a strong odor.

A low-quality diet can predispose a ferret to poor health, and, in extreme cases, cause nutritional deficiencies and disease. Low-quality food could cause a dull coat, excessive dryness and itchiness to the skin, lack of energy and larger than normal, wet, poorly formed, smelly stools.

☞ **_WARNING_** Do not buy foods that contain large amounts of plant protein such as soy flour, corn or gluten meal and dyes. Ferrets need meat-based protein. Do not buy foods that contain large amounts of fiber (vegetables and grains). Ferrets do not digest fiber well because they have a short large intestine and no cecum (a gut pocket to digest fiber). Excessive amounts of fiber lead to mucousy, soft stools.

☞ **_NOTE_** Feed your ferret only dry food unless there is a medical reason to do otherwise. Dry food also helps keep the ferret's teeth in good condition.

Anytime you change your ferret's diet, mix the original diet with the new diet for a few days to avoid diarrhea and other digestive upsets.

On a rare occasion a ferret may become obese. If you notice this happening, see your veterinarian. It could be an enlarged abdomen due to illness or simply winter weight gain.

Ferrets tend not to eat foods that smell fishy. Ferrets naturally are not fish-eaters, although some high-quality foods do contain a small amount of fish such as herring meal. The fish is used in small amounts to help balance the amino acids (building blocks of proteins).

Purchase the freshest foods. Store open food bags in an airtight container to prevent rancidity. Store the container in a cool, dry place such as a refrigerator. Never place any food directly on the floor. This encourages dampness, mold and insects.

TREATS

Ferrets love to snack on foods such as fruits and vegetables. However, they digest fiber poorly. What goes in as broccoli will come out as broccoli. Give treats in small amounts. Ferrets will stash excess food in hard-to-reach areas. Keep snack portions easily edible because ferrets may choke on larger pieces of food.

Some Of The Best Treats Are:

- 👍 1 tsp. finely chopped melon (no seeds, please)
- 👍 4-6 sugar- and salt-free Cheerios
- 👍 1 tsp. of chopped broccoli
- 👍 1 tsp. of chopped cucumber without the skin
- 👍 1 tsp. of chopped green pepper
- 👍 1 Tbsp. of whole cooked egg
- 👍 1 Tbsp. of cooked meat (especially chicken liver)
- 👍 1 Tbsp. of goat's milk

Ferrets have no self-control when they like a treat. Therefore, it is up to you to exercise a little discipline. Too many treats will lead to an unhealthy ferret. DON'T KILL THEM WITH KINDNESS!

Do Not Give Your Ferret The Following:

- Raw meat or eggs (They can contain harmful bacteria.)
- Dog food (It does not meet a ferret's nutritional needs. It is too high in ash, too low in animal protein and fat, and has too much plant protein.)
- Chocolate (It is toxic.)
- Dairy products such as ice cream or cheese (They can cause diarrhea.)
- Sweets (They can lead to diabetes.)
- Salty foods (They can lead to fluid retention in the body.)
- Bones (They can cause intestinal blockage and possible death.)
- Vegetarian cat food diets (Ferrets fed a vegetarian diet eventually will develop signs of malnutrition.)
- Alcoholic and carbonated beverages

SUPPLEMENTS

Ferrets sometimes need extra fat in their diet, especially during the winter months in the colder parts of the country. Additional fat can be added to the diet by using fatty acid supplements such as Linatone for cats (Lambert Kay) or Ferretone (8 in 1 Pet Products), available through your veterinarian or pet store. These products can be used daily up to 1/8 tsp. on a spoon or plate, perhaps at snack time.

☛ **WARNING** EXCESSIVE SUPPLEMENTS CAN DO MORE HARM THAN GOOD TO A FERRET! USE THEM ONLY AS DIRECTED BY YOUR FERRET'S VETERINARIAN!

Ferret-Proofing

Ferrets love to explore. And, more often than not, they can get into trouble because they truly live in the moment. Usually by the time ferrets are in trouble, it is too late. The problem is they SELDOM make an "alarm call" when they are injured and NEVER make an "alarm call" when they are lost. YOU have to do everything possible to keep THEM out of trouble.

Just remember that some of their favorite hiding places are UNDER THINGS and IN HOLES. They like to go to sleep in hard-to-reach areas. Do not assume that an opening is TOO SMALL for your ferret to get into. If it can get its head through a hole, it probably will get its body through, too, maybe with your car keys in tow! For this reason, you MUST anticipate escapes and ferret-proof your home BEFORE letting your ferret out to play.

SOME DANGER AREAS ARE:

Holes wider than an inch in diameter. These include openings in or around:

- Dishwashers

- Dryer vents

- Refrigerators

- Stoves

- Air-conditioning ducts

- Furnaces

- Window & door screens

- Walls & Floors

- Stairwells

- Forced-air heating grates that are not secured

- Plumbing pipes such as those under kitchen and bathroom cabinets

- Anywhere else that seems like a hiding place. CHECK AND BLOCK ANY HOLES WIDER THAN 1" IN DIAMETER. Get down on your hands and knees to look.

Recliners & Sofa Beds

Ferrets usually crawl inside for naps and get crushed when the chair is opened. GET RID OF RECLINERS AND CONVERTIBLE SOFAS OR MAKE THE ROOM(S) THEY ARE IN OFF-LIMITS!

Couches, Chairs & Mattresses

Ferrets have suffocated under chair and couch cushions and between mattresses. They also get under and burrow into this furniture. They often will eat the foam rubber stuffing. To prevent burrowing, attach hardware cloth or a thin board such as masonite underneath.

Kitchen & Bathroom Cabinets

USE CHILD-PROOF LATCHES TO SECURE CABINETS where garden chemicals, household cleaning products, poisons such as mouse bait, roach motels, insecticides and mouse traps are stored. You will not believe a ferret's resourcefulness until you see it open a cabinet door!

When moving into a new home or apartment be sure to look behind all appliances and in all cabinets for poisons left by previous owners.

Clothes Hampers

They are perfect hiding places. DO NOT PUT CLOTHES IN THE WASHER WITHOUT CHECKING THEM FIRST! Another favored sleep hide-out is under or inside clothes left on the floor. You do not want to suffer the consequences of accidentally stepping on your ferret!

Carpet Powders

They may cause irritation to the ferret's chin when it rubs on the carpet. The perfume and fine dust also may cause irritation to the respiratory tract.

Carpet Digging

Ferrets love to dig. If you have carpeting, especially next to the door - dig they must! You have two options: Remove the carpet or go to the hardware store and buy a plastic carpet runner. Do not declaw a ferret. (See Do Not Declaw That Paw, p. 97.)

The Innocent Ferret

Household Plants

Keep these out of reach. Ferrets rarely chew on plants (which may be poisonous) but there is always one ferret that will be an exception to the rule. All ferrets will enjoy digging in the dirt.

Stereo Speakers

Keep these out of reach. If your ferret gets inside, it probably will tear them apart. It also may chew on and swallow some of the materials.

Electrical Wires

Some ferrets like to chew on these and could be electrocuted.

Electric Floor Fans

Keep fans out of reach.

Open Doors

I cannot stress this enough. KEEP ALL DOORS TO THE OUTSIDE CLOSED! If your ferret gets out, you may never see it again.

Open Windows

Ferrets can climb. Be certain that all open windows are out of reach. Ferrets can claw their way through and out window screens. A ferret can get its nail caught in window screening, tearing out one or two nails trying to get loose.

Sliding Glass Doors

Lock or put hooks on all sliding glass doors. Some ferrets will learn how to open them. Balconies should be off-limits. Ferrets have poor eyesight and may go over the edge.

Staircases

Ferrets love running up and down stairs. An open stairway can be dangerous.

Bathrooms

If your ferret falls into a bathtub filled with water, it easily will tire trying to escape and probably drown. Also be sure to keep all toilet lids down.

Most Commonly Ingested Foreign Materials & Liquids:

- Anything made from vinyl, soft rubber (i.e. latex toys) or plastics

- Foam rubber soles and insoles of shoes

- Styrofoam or packing material

- Sponges

- Refrigerator & pipe insulation (under bathroom and kitchen sinks)

- Cotton balls

- Rubber bands

- Electrical cords

- Holiday decorations such as snow spray, Christmas tree preservative solutions, mistletoe berries and tinsel.

- Antifreeze

Keep in mind that ferrets are ground-dwelling animals and even though they are afraid of and confused by heights they aimlessly will explore them. Unaware of the dangers, some have been known to climb window screens and curtains and fall. The result could be a broken back, limbs, concussion or fatal, internal bleeding.

My ferrets Twiggy and Newfy often climb onto a couch then try to hop onto a nearby table. If they successfully judge the distance, both usually walk or roughhouse their way over the edge of the table.

After the shock of the fall is over, they foolishly climb back up and next time poorly estimate the distance between the table and the couch. Both come crashing to the floor. Supervision is a must!

Ferrets (especially ferrets wearing collars with bells) sometimes can get themselves wedged between two objects or inside objects.

To illustrate this point, recently I was preparing dinner in the kitchen when I heard a loud, thumping sound. When I turned to look, there was Twiggy, backing across the floor with her head stuck inside a small, glass juice bottle. How did it happen? Well, somehow Twigg got into my recycling bin and you know the rest...

I took her, bottle in one hand, hips in the other, placed her in my lap, put some olive oil around her neck and gently pulled her head out. Twigg frequently gets into trouble.

Escapes & Captures

Ferrets love to explore and hide. They will take any presented opportunity to slip out of the house. If by some chance you or someone else have left an outside door open for more than a few seconds and suddenly you cannot find your ferret, what should you do?

Immediately go through every area of your home calling your ferret's name and squeezing its special toy. (See Loud, Squeaky Toy, p. 54.) If your ferret is sleeping, the noise of the toy normally will wake it up. Look inside drawers, under dressers, under and inside couches, in closets, hampers, suitcases stored in closets, kitchen trash cans, tubes connected to vacuum cleaners, behind refrigerators, and check dryer vents.

If you cannot find your ferret in the house, check all around the outside. Look in garages, sheds; check bushes and under the house; look inside the car (including under the hood).

Pick up all mouse, mole, ant and cockroach traps or insecticides that may be outside your home, sheds or garages.

Speak to your neighbors and ask them to be on the lookout. Take a recent photo of your ferret with you since they may not know what one is or what it looks like. Ferrets often are mistaken for mink or rats and sometimes they are chased, beaten with brooms or shot to death. Ask permission to check your neighbors' sheds, garages and, possibly, dryer vents.

☞ **NOTE** It is a good idea to let your neighbors know that you have a ferret and what it looks like BEFORE something happens. IF your little MUNCHKIN should sneak out and go next door, your neighbors will know to call you.

Place a cage outside your home. Put food and water along with your ferret's favorite blanket and toy inside.

Go around your neighborhood calling your ferret's name and squeaking the loud, squeaky toy every 15-30 minutes. Ferrets have been known to go into a deep sleep under houses. The toy and/or your voice may be able to wake it up.

Place notices with a photo of your ferret along with your phone number on street corners in your neighborhood, at grocery stores and gas stations. Put an ad in the local newspaper. Offer a reward.

Call your local ferret club, local veterinary offices, the Humane Society, Animal Control, and wildlife center to report your ferret missing. Give them a description of your ferret along with your name and phone number. Remember to call back frequently.

Alert your mail carrier, newspaper delivery person and anyone else who regularly visits your area.

Keep a recent photo of your ferret handy, showing its colors and special markings in case you are asked to identify your pet. Remember that mask conformation and coat may change with seasons and age.

IF YOU ARE NOT SUCCESSFUL IN FINDING YOUR LOST FERRET, THIS WILL BE AN INCREDIBLY PAINFUL LESSON ABOUT KEEPING DOORS CLOSED AND BLOCKING OTHER POSSIBLE ESCAPE ROUTES.

Chapter 5
HANDLING & SOCIALIZING

Now You're Home

Once you have visited the veterinarian, purchased all ferret necessities and you are all safe and snug at home, it is time to relax. Right? Wrong! If your new ferret is a kit, you now have the equivalent of a 2-year-old child. This child is going to want to make its own rules. Forget the cuddling, this "toddler" is going to want to play, play, play and explore, explore, explore! Young ferrets do not like to be restrained.

They are full of boundless energy. They will entertain you for hours. While you work on training them, they will be working on training you! Just remember that ferrets begin to mature at 6 months, so there IS light at the end of the tunnel.

If your ferret is older, it probably will not be as rambunctious, but it will be just as much fun. Mature ferrets slow down a bit, but they are still just as lovable and curious. In fact, one of the joys of ferret ownership is that, unlike mature cats and dogs, ferrets NEVER lose their playfulness. No matter how old they are, ferrets need lots of love and companionship.

Bonding With Your Ferret

Bonding is a process that will require time, nurturing and plenty of patience.

Consider the first month to be a sensitive time for your new pet. The ferret will have to adapt to a new environment. Shy or nervous ferrets will need extra time. It is crucial to allow the pet to adapt at its own speed.

First, create an area in your home that is to be the ferret's separate domain, a place where your ferret can establish its own boundaries and go when it is hungry, thirsty, tired, scared or perhaps wants to be alone.

☞ **NOTE** Until the ferret has completed its necessary vaccinations, you need to restrict it from other pets, people and keep it inside.

Even though your first instinct probably will be to take your new pet out and play with it, don't! Let your ferret's first day at home be a quiet one, allowing your pet to adapt to its cage environment. It is important for the ferret to first feel secure in its own home. Your best course of action is to let the ferret investigate its cage, including the litter box. Then let it take a nap, eat and relieve itself before taking it out. Begin with short handling sessions, then increase the time as the ferret feels at home.

By the way, do not expect a neat and clean cage the first 2-3 days. The ferret will rearrange and root through everything, including the litter pan until it adapts to its new home.

If you have not yet purchased a cage (See photo, A Suitable Cage, p. 49), keep the ferret confined to a small area at first. A ferret-proofed bathroom would be ideal. If you give it free run of your home, it will be overwhelmed and difficult to litter-train.

☞ **NOTE** Ferret-proof the confined area. Check to see that the ferret cannot open cabinets or wiggle under the door. Stick-on or screw-on door strips can be purchased at most hardware stores if the space between door and floor is more than 1/2".

Since its vision is limited, ALWAYS SPEAK TO YOUR FERRET IN A GENTLE TONE OF VOICE BEFORE YOU PICK IT UP. This will not only let it know you are approaching, but will let it become familiar with your voice and its name.

A ferret's skeletal structure is fragile, so HOW you pick it up is important. Always lift from behind using two hands - one supporting its chest; the other cradling its hips.

NEVER PICK UP A FERRET BY ITS TAIL!! NEVER GRAB YOUR FERRET UNEXPECTEDLY!! BE CAREFUL NOT TO MAKE ANY SUDDEN MOVEMENTS TOWARDS YOUR FERRET!! It may become nervous and nip if you do. Let the little one come to you. It will let you know when it wants to be picked up by holding onto your leg or grabbing your wrist when you extend your hand.

It is also a good idea to teach your children and friends not to grab at the ferret either. Love and consideration are the best "buddy" makers.

Playtime

The ferret's capacity for delight can only bring you joy. These little bundles of energy will capture your heart, stimulate your imagination and test your stamina and willingness to endure their childlike antics.

You will find that you, yes, you, are a fundamental part of a ferret's fun time. No matter how many toys or animal companions they have, they want to spend at least 50 percent of their playtime with human companions. Play provides a source of exercise and helps socialize the ferret.

Ferrets often will dance around you, hug your ankles or wrists or even gently nip at you to let you know they are ready for some one-on-one quality time.

Ferrets seem to know exactly what they are not allowed to do. Saying "NO" will be interpreted as "do it again". My Twigg and Newfy used to love to hear the telephone ring. For them it was an opportunity to nose about forbidden territory. I no longer answer the phone at playtime.

I have never known of any other domesticated pet to spend so much time trying to outsmart an owner or caretaker.

Exercising Your Ferret

I have purchased a toy chest just for my ferrets. In it I have 12 small, hard rubber balls with a bell inside, an extra large pair of men's blue jeans, a dryer vent hose (25 ft.), 3 paper bags and flying toys such as feathers attached to string on a pole (resembling a fishing pole).

The Treasure Chest

Each and every morning I take everything out. I spread out the blue jeans on the floor and extend the dryer vent hose throughout a large room around the furniture. The balls and the flying toys I keep for our one-on-one playtime.

I open the cage door and out come my little rascals. Newfy goes directly into the dryer hose. Twiggy bolts for the kitchen. She refuses to play until she has had at least 3 treats.

After a quick breakfast with Twigg, Newfy is ready for his exercise routine. That's where the small, hard rubber balls come into play.

I sit on the floor and rattle the balls. Newfy comes running, Twigg just hangs out and waits for her exercise routine; she is not a fetcher. I throw a ball, one by one, close to the floor across the room. Newfy makes a mad dash to fetch the ball. Once he catches the ball he manages to hold it in his little mouth then runs to his bedroom to hide it. He quickly returns for his next fetch. Twelve balls later, he has run his ferret mile and is flaked out on the floor.

Next I get the flying feather toy. While Newfy rests, Twigg runs, jumps and dances about trying to catch the feathers. Within 10 minutes she is flaked out on the floor.

After they both have had their time-out, they explore and playfight inside the blue jeans, the paper bags and they run in and out of the dryer hose chasing each other. Within an hour and a half, Twiggy goes back to her cage, runs upstairs, gets in her hammock and goes to sleep. Newfy drags the blue jeans under the dresser, gets inside and naps until I put him in his cage for safekeeping. When both are safely tucked away, I collect their toys and put them back in their treasure chest. Twigg and Newfy play twice a day.

☞ **WARNING** If you have children, explain to them the dangers toddler toys and "big-kid" toys can pose to ferrets. Show them what may be broken or chewed off a child's toy and swallowed; or what is small enough to pose a choking threat.

Keep all children's toys out of reach. Ferrets will remember where something is stored. They will try opening closet doors or climbing. They will try, try and try again.

Understanding Animal Behavior

By nature, animals are limited by their instinct. They cannot reason. They do not know right from wrong. An animal's inborn response to a situation always is spontaneous and its behavior is determined by what is happening at the moment and in the environment in which the animal is present.

An animal verbally cannot tell you when it is hungry, feeling abused, scared, tired, ill or in pain or when it has been injured. The means of communication in these circumstances sometimes are through the use of their jaws or claws.

Veterinarians clearly understand that even the sweetest, most gentle pet is capable of biting or scratching when it feels violated.

Domesticated animals learn trust from trustworthy caretakers. If a pet is mistreated it will develop a sense of distrust. The animal must be on guard and be in control. Fear moves animals to act out in the face of danger.

Baby Safety Tips

Ferrets, like cats and dogs, have been known to seriously injure babies through scratches and bites.

If there is a baby in your home, make certain that all your pets have a complete medical examination. Be sure that rabies shots are up to date and that the pets are flea-and tick-free.

Keep the ferret in its cage until its playtime. Allow your pet to play in a separate area of your home, away from the baby.

Most safety gates will not prevent a ferret from entering a baby's room or a child's play area. Ferrets easily can climb over the gate or slide through small holes.

Do place a gate to block the ferret's room while the ferret is in its cage. When the baby learns to crawl, the little one will not be able to poke its fingers in the ferret's cage or have access to ferret food and water.

Toddler Safety Tips

A baby ferret and a toddler equal double trouble. Both naturally will test their limits and require a lot of attention and training.

Do You Have Enough Time In Your Schedule For Two Toddlers?

A pet ferret cannot be toddler-trained. Since ferrets, other pets and toddlers can be unpredictable, strict supervision is recommended at all times. The potential for harm (intentional or not) is great on both sides. If the two are together, keep the getting-to-know-each-other sessions brief at first so neither the ferret nor the toddler is overwhelmed. Toddlers can create a bite situation, even though they mean to show affection. Supervise, supervise, supervise.

While it is true young children can learn many lessons from animals, it also is true animals need to be cared for by responsible adults and children.

Teach your children that pets are not stuffed toys. Instruct children to follow these safety guidelines:

THE "NEVERS"

- *Never* go near any animal without a grown-up around.
- *Never* open up a pet's cage without a grown-up around.
- *Never* move quickly toward an animal.
- *Never* go near animals when they are fighting.
- *Never* wake up a sleeping pet.
- *Never* scream in a pet's ear.
- *Never* put your face next to a pet's face.
- *Never* kick, hit or bite a pet.
- *Never* tease a pet.
- *Never* chase a pet around the house.
- *Never* poke fingers in a pet's cage.
- *Never* poke fingers in a pet's eyes, pull on its tail or fur, pick it up by the tail, tug on its ears or step on the pet.
- *Never* feed a pet any treats unless given permission by the owner.
- *Never* eat the pet's food.
- *Never* eat the pet's hair.
- *Never* let a pet lick an open wound.
- *Never* put fingers in the mouth after touching or cleaning up after a pet. Wash hands first.

☞ **WARNING** Never leave an infant, small child or persons incapable of defending themselves, such as the handicapped or elderly, alone with any animal, no matter how well you think you know the pet or the individual. Ferrets and very young children simply do not mix and are not recommended. The No. 1 cause of bites by pets inflicted on children is the lack of parental supervision.

☞ **NOTE** Do not buy a ferret (or any pet) to teach a child responsibility. Buy a ferret for a RESPONSIBLE child.

Remember, once you have learned how to handle your ferret, it is crucial that you teach your children how to handle and treat it properly, too.

Tommy & His Friend

Ferrets & Nipping

A nipping kit is an emerging adventurer with new chompers. The baby ferret playfully will test his new instruments out on your toes, ankles, fingers or any other part that happens to be in its way.

Ferrets have thick skin covered with fur. It's natural for kits to playfight with each other, not feel pain, and come out without a scratch. (See Predatory Behavior, p. 21.) But our thin skin feels those sharp, little teeth, and, boy, can they hurt.

As your ferret grows from babyhood to toddlerhood (still nipping), it eventually will outgrow the nipping stage. Into adulthood and through-out its life, your ferret, on occasion, still may nip for attention, a treat, or to simply say "I am the boss."

As you play with your ferret, do not allow your ferret to continually nip at your ankles (their favorite place), your hands, or anywhere else. Roughhousing and allowing the ferret to nip you on occasion encour-ages the animal into nipping you painfully hard.

☞ **NOTE** Never flick or hit a ferret (or any pet) for nipping. It will only make the ferret nervous or angry and it may then bite out of fear. If a child sees you yelling at or hitting an animal, the child undoubtedly will repeat this abusive behavior on your pet and potentially on someone else's pet, possibly creating a bite situ-ation. Violence breeds violence! Studies unequivocally have shown that what a child learns most likely will be practiced as an adult.

The most effective way to respond to a nip is to grasp the ferret by the scruff of the neck, calmly remove it, then look into its eyes and say "NO!" loudly. (This works for me.) Then quickly divert the ferret's attention elsewhere, such as playing with a toy. This is a natural, nonpainful form of punishment.

You may have to repeat this several times until the ferret learns who is the boss. It is up to you to teach your pet acceptable behavior. Ferrets have no idea their playful nipping behavior is hurting you. The ferret will need to learn playful nipping is for its animal companions.

An excellent aid to prevent nipping is a product such as Bitter Lime (Four Paws) to train a ferret to not bite. It can be sprayed on your hands prior to handling. It can be put on socks and shoes for those "ankle nippers." It also can be sprayed along the neck and back of ferrets to prevent fighting (when introducing a new one). And finally, it can be sprayed on the mouth of a ferret that is "hanging" onto you. They hate the taste and it is nontoxic. However, use sparingly and be careful not to spray it into the ferret's eyes.

☛ **WARNING** The only times a ferret may bite are when it has not been properly socialized, it is starving, terrified, neglected or abused, injured, ill or in pain. ANY ANIMAL WOULD DO THE SAME! Any pet that bites out of fear is in a moment of panic.

Tommy & His Pals

CHAPTER 6
HOUSEBREAKING

How To Litter-Train Your Ferret

The time has arrived to get down to the nitty-gritty of litter-training. If you have ever housebroken a dog, the method is similar. Positive reinforcement and repetition are the keys to success. Patience is the name of the game.

New ferret owners tend to keep their animals too confined at first or give them free run of the house. You do not want to do either.

EXPAND YOUR FERRET'S PLAY AREA ONE ROOM AT A TIME. Your ferret is going to want to choose its own corners in each room and rarely will return to the cage to use the litter pan.

WHERE TO START...
A small, confined area such as a cage or a bathroom, but for our purposes here, let's assume you are using the cage.

WHAT YOU WILL NEED...
A litter pan about 4"-5" high. Cut one side of the container down if your ferret has difficulty getting in. If your pet misses and does its business over the side, the sides of the pan need to be higher. It is wise to secure the pan because your ferret may move it around.

Use 1" of litter (more if needed). Your ferret probably will play or sleep in the litter until it learns how to use the pan as a toilet.

WHAT TO DO...

Put the pan in a CORNER of the cage. Then fill the remaining corners with bedding and food dishes. Ferrets are very clean. They will not want to soil their bedding or dirty where they eat.

When your ferret wants to relieve itself, it usually will start sniffing around for a corner. Once it finds a corner, it will turn around, back into it with its hind area and tail raised and go. If you watch closely, you will begin to recognize this behavior. PUT YOUR FERRET IN THE LITTER PAN WHEN YOU SEE IT SNIFFING AROUND. TIMING IS EVERYTHING. IF YOU WAIT UNTIL IT TURNS AROUND TO BACK UP - TOO LATE!

Your ferret usually will relieve itself soon after waking from a nap and will poop several times during the day IN THE SAME CORNER. Remember, what a ferret eats will pass through it in approximately 3-4 hours.

POOP GOES THE WEASEL

Unlike cats, ferrets do not cover their "business," so you will more than likely want to scoop twice a day. But always leave a little residue until your ferret knows where to find its "toilet."

☞ **NOTE** Once or twice a week, change the litter and wash the pan. If you do not keep your ferret's litter pan clean, your ferret may relieve itself on the floor next to the pan. Remember to save a little of the ferret's "business" to put in the clean litter pan to remind the ferret the pan is its toilet - not its play box.

LITTER PAN PLACEMENT

Be aware that after your ferret has done its "business" in the pan, it will jump out and proceed to drag its rear end across the floor 3"-6" from the pan or 3"-6" from its chosen corner. This is known as the "anal wipe". The ferret is simply wiping its rear end.

Placing a litter pan on your favorite carpet without protection from the ferret's "anal wipe" is not a good idea.

Do not place the pan near a furnace, radiator, washer, dryer or anything else capable of making loud noises. Your ferret may choose a more serene location.

A HELPFUL TECHNIQUE

Place a piece of newspaper in each available corner of a room until your ferret chooses the one it wants. It is a good idea to secure the paper to the corner with tape because the ferret will think of it as another toy and crawl under it. Make sure to extend 3" of the paper up the wall to protect it. It also helps to place some ferret poop on the paper in the corner. Then take the ferret over to the paper and let it smell the scent so it will know that this is a possible toilet area.

Once the ferret has chosen its corner, remove the soiled portion of the paper and put it in the litter pan. Then cover the soiled paper with litter and put the pan in the corner where the newspaper was.

When the ferret looks like it has to go again, IMMEDIATELY AND REPEATEDLY put it in the pan until it goes. Most will learn right away, but some need to be reminded. Ferrets are creatures of habit so this will work in your favor for litter-training. Once your pet has learned what to do, it will do it again. To be effective, I would recommend reminding your ferret where its litter pan is for at least 3-4 weeks.

☞ **NOTE** When you first let your ferret out to play, immediately put it into the litter pan to remind it where to find its toilet. After the ferret has been out playing awhile, again remind it where its toilet is by placing it in the litter pan.

☞ **SPECIAL NOTE** Do not rub the ferret's nose in its business, yell at it for making a mistake or hit the ferret with your hand or anything else. This violent behavior only will cause anxiety, which may result in aggressive behavior. Successful housebreaking with any pet takes time. Consistent behavior and kindness will help it learn best.

Ferrets rarely use a litter pan outside their cage 100% of the time. My ferrets make a mistake at least once a day. It is not a big deal, I simply clean it up. I then spray the area with a pure, natural odor eliminator.

☞ **NOTE** Once litter-trained, if your ferret stops using the pan, it is usually because...

♦ The ferret is in a new environment.

♦ The ferret's chosen corner has been filled with furniture.

♦ The pan is dirty.

♦ Food and water may be placed too close to the pan.

♦ The ferret is angry with you.

♦ The ferret has picked up a bad habit from a newcomer that is not yet litter-trained.

- The ferret is refusing to share its litter pan with a newly arrived playmate.

- The ferret is sick.

- Aging ferrets (4 years and older) sometimes will lose their pan-training habits. Ferrets may become weak in the hind legs as they age. Make sure they easily can get in and out of their litter boxes.

Incidentally, if you are holding your ferret and it starts to squirm more than usual, it probably has to use the litter pan.

Abnormal Stools

The digestive system breaks food down into nutrients to be absorbed by the body. The waste material is excreted through the anus. The ferret's digestive system includes the mouth, esophagus, stomach, small intestine, large intestine and rectum.

The digestive tract is subject to various disorders such as:

- Gastrointestinal foreign bodies (ingested, indigestible material such as rubber, vinyl, plastic or foam rubber)

- Parasites

- Bacterial diseases

- Viral diseases

- Cancer

- Toxin ingestion

- Stomach ulcers

Healthy stools are soft yet shaped, and when left to dry, turn dark and hard. If you notice any of the following abnormal signs, take your ferret to the veterinarian.

WARNING SIGNS

◆ Blood in stool ◆ Black, tarry or sticky stool ◆ Green, soft stool ◆ Excessive mucus in stool (clear or green) ◆ Diarrhea ◆ No stool for 12 hours or longer ◆ Foreign objects in stool ◆ Worms in stool ◆

☞ **NOTE** Do not give anti-diarrheal medications without instructions from your veterinarian.

Abnormal Urination

The ferret's urinary system is designed to remove various toxic wastes from its body. The system consists of the kidneys, ureters, bladder and urethra.

The urinary tract is subject to various diseases such as:

- ◆ Bacterial infections
- ◆ Bladder stones
- ◆ Cancer of the bladder or kidneys
- ◆ Polycystic kidneys

If you notice any of the following abnormal signs, take your ferret to the veterinarian.

WARNING SIGNS

◆ Inability or straining to urinate ◆ Frequent urination ◆ Blood in urine ◆ Pus or sandy material in urine ◆ Crying when urinating ◆ Loss of bladder control ◆ Strong-smelling urine ◆ Greenish-colored urine ◆

Chapter 7
A GUIDE TO GROOMING

Bathing Your Ferret

Ferrets are fastidiously clean animals. Unfortunately, that has no bearing on their love of bathing. Few ever take kindly to or enjoy a bath. WHEN your ferret needs a bath is totally dependent on YOU and YOUR ferret. In other words, some may bathe their ferret every 2 weeks, some once a month, some a few times a year and others never at all. DO NOT BATHE YOUR FERRET MORE THAN ONCE A WEEK! Excessive bathing will strip the skin and fur of its essential oils, leading to a dry, itchy condition.

If you live in a cold climate, you may need to give baths less often. Use a conditioner that is made for kittens/cats or ferrets to prevent skin and coat dryness.

If you have more than one ferret, make it easy on yourself. Bathe them one at a time. Never leave your ferret unattended in a sink or bathtub.

YOU WILL NEED:

- ♦ Kitten/cat or ferret shampoo
- ♦ Cotton swabs
- ♦ A warm towel
- ♦ Veterinary-approved ear cleanser

☞ **NOTE** DO NOT use a shampoo that is labeled "For Dogs Only." DO NOT use human shampoos. The skin of ferrets is less acidic than that of humans. Human shampoo can irritate and dry out the skin and fur of your pet.

If your ferret has not relieved itself prior to bathing, it may in its excitement, do its "business" in the bath water.

What To Do...

♦ HAVE EVERYTHING READY BEFORE you bring your ferret to the basin. This should include filling the basin with 2"-3" of warm (not hot) water. (Not too much water, you do not want to drown the little MUNCHKIN.) Some ferrets do not like the sound of running water.

♦ HOLD your ferret gently and securely as you slowly put it into the water. If your ferret is frightened, you may want to try speaking to it in a gentle tone of voice.

♦ BEGIN by soaking your ferret. Then lather it up starting at the head, working your way down through the tail. Be careful not to get soap or water up its nose, in its eyes or in the ears. Some ferrets will like the taste of shampoo - don't let them eat any because they may get sick.

♦ MOISTEN a cotton swab with ear cleanser and carefully clean each ear. DO NOT GO INTO THE EAR CANAL. (See Ears, p. 90.)

♦ RINSE by running clean, warm water over the ferret. Then you should gently squeeze the excess water from its fur and tail.

♦ PRE-DRY the ferret with a warm towel.

When you have finished, the ferret should be placed in a warm, dry area. Give your little character a fresh, dry towel and watch it play. Ferrets get pretty frisky after a bath! DO NOT return the ferret to its cage until it is completely dry. When your ferret is dry, give it 1/2" of cat hairball laxative. (See Fur, p. 100.)

NOT MY BATH TIME, IT'S TWIGGY'S!

HI, I'M SAM.

1. Wash

CHECK YOUR FERRET'S SKIN ON A REGULAR BASIS FOR DRYNESS, SCABS, ULCERS, LUMPS OR LITTLE BLACK SPECKS OF FLEA FECES.

2. Rinse

3. Dry

PRE-DRY THE FERRET
WITH A WARM TOWEL;
PLACE THE FERRET IN
A DRY AREA TO LET IT
FINISH THE GROOMING
PROCESS.

4. Give 1/2" OF HAIRBALL LAXATIVE TO PREVENT HAIRBALLS.

TWIGGY DID NOT ENJOY HER
BATH TODAY. NOTICE THE
BOTTLE BRUSH TAIL.

TWIGGY LICKING UP HER LAXATIVE.

ODOR CONTROL

My female, Twigg, is spayed and my male, Newfy, is neutered. And because I bathe them every 2 weeks, give them clean bedding every 3 days, provide them with a high-quality diet, keep the litter box clean and give them a stress-free life... my ferrets virtually are odor-free!!

If you find the slight, musky odor offensive, you might consider purchasing a portable air cleaner. It will remove odors, pollen, dust mites, allergens, dander, mold spores and fumes from the air. You can install an air filter/cleaner (permanent filter that fits into the heating/cooling system in place of a regular filter). You also can remove carpeting from ferret areas.

☞ **NOTE** If you ARE doing all these things and there is still a strong odor, your pet may have a medical problem. See your veterinarian as soon as possible.

Ears

It is recommended that you check your ferret's ears at least once a week and clean as needed with a cotton swab moistened with a veterinary-approved ear cleanser. AVOID INSERTING COTTON SWABS DEEP INTO THE EAR CANAL BECAUSE YOU MAY DAMAGE THE EARDRUM. By checking the ears and keeping them clean and dry, you can prevent any problem from becoming chronic.

It is normal to have a small amount of reddish-brown ear wax in the ears all of the time. It is protective. It is NOT necessary to remove all of the wax.

☞ **NOTE** You can use a small amount of peroxide occasionally. Do not use alcohol because it can cause dryness and will sting if there are any cuts or scratches on the outer ear.

How To Clean...

♦ START by pouring a little ear cleanser into a small container and have cotton swabs ready to clean the outer ear.

♦ GRASP your ferret by the scruff (loose area of skin on the back of the neck, between the ears and shoulder blades). (See photo, p. 92.)

♦ SUPPORT the ferret on a counter top.

♦ PUT a few drops of cleaning solution into the ferret's ears. Gently massage the ears to soften and loosen the material in the ear canal. The ferret probably will shake its head, bringing the debris to the outer part of the ear.

♦ DIP the cotton swab in the solution. Use the wet side of the swab to clean the outermost portions of the ear canal and ear flap. Then use the dry side to soak up excess moisture.

♦ REPEAT as needed, using fresh cotton swabs.

☞ **NOTE** Ferrets can develop tumors in or on their ears. They also are susceptible to ear mites and ear infections. Any of these conditions left untreated can lead to serious problems. If you have more than one ferret, all will need to be checked because mites may spread from ferret to ferret and to other household pets.

WARNING SIGNS

♦ Growth on ear ♦ Odor ♦ Ear discharge ♦ Inflamed ears ♦ Excessive reddish-brown or black wax in ears ♦ Ferret scratching its ears or shaking its head ♦ Rubbing ears against the floor ♦ Persistent head tilting ♦

☞ **NOTE** If your pet is showing any of the above signs, do not clean the ears without instruction from your pet's veterinarian. If your ferret is prescribed ear medication, clean ears before administering the medication.

IT'S TWIGGY'S NAIL-CUTTING TIME.

ME, AGAIN!

INTRODUCING TWIGGY TO LINATONE

SCRUFFING TWIGGY

METHOD 2 - TRIMMING TWIGGY'S NAILS.

TWIGGY ENJOYING THE LINATONE

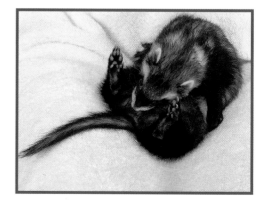

NEWFY IS ENJOYING HIS DAILY GROOMING

INGESTED HAIR CAN CAUSE HAIRBALLS.

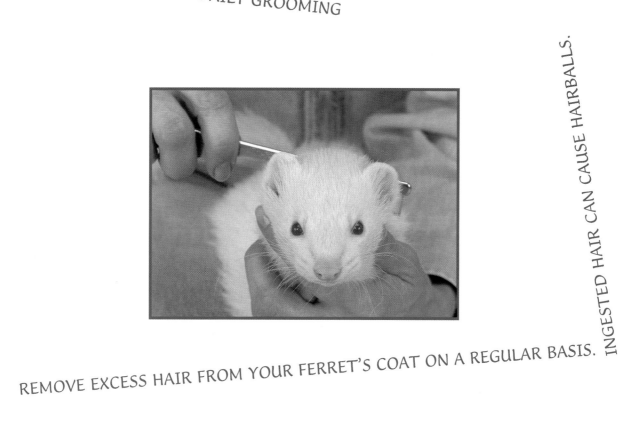

REMOVE EXCESS HAIR FROM YOUR FERRET'S COAT ON A REGULAR BASIS.

Nail Care

Proper nail care is an important part of your ferret's grooming program. Nails need to be clipped on a regular basis (7-10 days), not only to avoid your getting scratched, but as protection for the animal. Long nails can get caught in towels, bedding or carpeting and also place undue stress upon the joints of the paws.

WHEN AND HOW TO CUT THE NAILS...

The optimal time to do this is when your pet is tired or sleeping, NOT when it is at its friskiest. Natural daylight is best. If you do not have proper lighting, have someone shine a bright light (from a flashlight or pen light) on the nails.

Method 1

If you have someone who can help you, let him/her hold the animal while you do the clipping. To trim nails you will need a pair of human or cat clippers.

Your helper should grasp your ferret by the scruff of the neck and let it "dangle" in the air. Its lower body should be supported on a counter top or your helper's lap.

Before you start, take your ferret's paw, gently grasp the nail, and look for the pink blood vein area. It is easy to see with a bright light. YOU DO NOT WANT TO CUT INTO THE PINK AREA!! If you do, it will be painful and the vein will bleed. Accidents happen, of course, so if you should slip and nick the vein area, use a styptic powder, corn starch or cold water to stop the bleeding. Using a sterile gauze bandage or a clean cloth, apply direct pressure.

Method 2

To trim the nails you will need a pair of human or cat nail clippers. To aid in the clipping you will need a fatty acid supplement such as Linatone for cats or a cat hairball laxative.

Look at photos on p. 92 and illustrations below and on p. 96. Take your ferret, sit down, scruff it by the neck and place it in your lap. On the ferret's belly distribute 3 or 4 drops of Linatone. Next, take your scruffed ferret and put its nose to the Linatone. While your ferret is busy licking, cut its nails. Some ferrets eat faster than others. You may need to add a few more drops.

☞ **NOTE** If your ferret has never had Linatone before, introduce the ferret to the product before attempting to cut the nails.

You probably will notice that as your ferret gets older, its nails will start to curl. Therefore, keep its nails trimmed on a regular basis. If you do not, your ferret could become entangled in its bedding and remain there unable to reach its food and water until you come home.

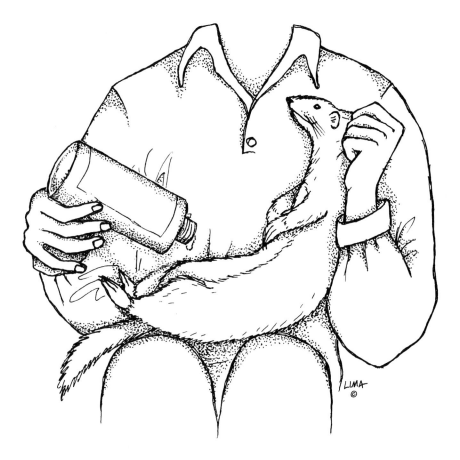

Method 2

Method 2

☞ **NOTE** If your ferret's nails get caught on anything (bedding, towels or carpeting), grasp it by the scruff of the neck, controlling its head, because it may bite if it is hurt or in pain. Free the nail and assess the damage.

Sometimes the ferret actually will tear the nail out near the nail bed. Your first concern is to stop the bleeding. Going to the veterinarian should be your next step because the ferret may need stitches or nail removal and antibiotics to prevent infection.

If your ferret's nail is simply broken or torn, clip off any hanging pieces and clean with hydrogen peroxide.

Paws and Pads

Once the nails have been trimmed, examine the paws and pads. They are vulnerable to injury and signs of illness.

WARNING SIGNS

♦ Bleeding pads ♦ Paws swollen and/or inflamed ♦ Ferret chewing on paws ♦ Thick paw pads ♦ Growth on paws ♦ Red, bluish, purple or pale pads ♦

Aging ferrets may have dry and thickened pads. Use a tiny bit of petroleum jelly on the pads to help ease the dryness.

☞ **NOTE** Unclean cages may lead to nail bed or foot infections. It is important to keep the cage clean.

Do Not Declaw That Paw

Declawing is a surgical procedure that involves the removal of the claw and the bone it is attached to. If not done properly, the claws grow back but are often deformed. Deformed claws can be more prone to infection. The ferret's claws are a gift of nature. Please do not make the animal suffer by taking them away.

Ferrets Need Their Nails For...

♦ Grasping onto objects and moving them around

♦ Climbing up on beds and couches and lowering themselves down

♦ Traction when they walk

♦ Digging and scratching, which serves to tone muscles

♦ Removing particles of food that sometimes get caught in the roof of their mouth

The Physical Effects Of Declawing A Ferret...

♦ Grasping ability would be damaged.

♦ Climbing would be out of the question.

♦ Balance is impaired

♦ The joy of digging and scratching would be gone.

♦ The ferret's ability to remove particles of food caught in the roof of the ferret's mouth would be difficult.

♦ Pain from the surgery

Teeth

Ferrets have 30 baby teeth, which will erupt between 20-28 days of age. They have 34 adult teeth, which will erupt between 50-74 days of age. The number and condition of the teeth can be used to estimate the age of a ferret.

There are 4 main types of teeth. The small upper and lower *incisors* located in the front are used to gather food. The *canines*, also called "fang" or "eye" teeth, are used to puncture the food. The upper and lower *premolars* are used to shear or cut food. The upper and lower *molars* are used to grind up food.

Have your veterinarian check your pet's teeth and clean them as needed. Routine cleaning is an effective means of preventive health care. General anesthesia is required. Dentistry is an important aspect of health care.

Do Not "Trim" Ferret Teeth

Ferrets occasionally are presented to veterinarians to "trim" teeth to decrease damage from biting. In most cases the veterinarian simply cuts the tooth in half. Unfortunately, this allows food and bacteria to travel down the open root canal system, eventually causing a deep infection. In addition to being painful, the infection also can spread to the heart, liver and kidneys. If your ferret's teeth have been trimmed in the past, a veterinarian familiar with dentistry should be consulted to X-ray the tooth roots and remove the infected nerve prior to sealing the canal if possible.

Skin

The skin, like the hair and nails, is in a constant state of growth. It regularly requires large amounts of nutrients. The skin provides an excellent window into your ferret's health. Any changes in the skin are a sign that something may be wrong. Check your ferret's skin on a regular basis for dryness, scabs, ulcers, lumps or little black specks of flea feces (dried digested blood).

WARNING SIGNS

♦ Scaly or crusty skin ♦ Scabs, rashes or sores that will not heal ♦ Growths, lumps or ulcers on any part of the body (including ears, feet and tail) ♦ Skin color changes such as yellow or deep red ♦

☞ **NOTE** Do not use a medicated shampoo without having the ferret's skin condition diagnosed by a veterinarian.

Prevention of Skin Dryness

♦ Feed your ferret a high-quality diet.

♦ Give your ferret up to 1/8 tsp. daily of a fatty acid supplement such as Linatone for cats. This will help produce more oils for the skin and fur. If the condition does not improve within 1-2 weeks, or if there is hair loss, take your pet to the veterinarian.

♦ Use a pet hair (coat and skin) conditioner when bathing.

♦ Use a humidifier in the room.

Fur

You already know that ferrets shed their winter coat for a summer coat. Shedding can cause problems, mainly hairballs. FERRETS DO NOT VOMIT UP HAIRBALLS AS CATS DO, THEREFORE, IT IS POSSIBLE FOR THE HAIRBALL TO CAUSE INTESTINAL BLOCKAGE AND DEATH.

WARNING SIGNS

♦ Poor or intermittent appetite ♦ Coughing ♦ Vomiting ♦ Weight loss ♦ Intermittent, tarry stools ♦ Sudden collapse ♦

If your ferret exhibits the above signs, immediately take it to the veterinarian. Your ferret may require life-saving surgery.

What To Do To Help Prevent Hairballs...

♦ Ask your veterinarian about using a cat hairball laxative.

♦ Give your ferret 1/2" of a cat hairball laxative 2-3 times a week and after its bath, to help your ferret clear its digestive tract of any hair that might have been swallowed.

♦ Brush your ferret daily with a soft brush or use a flea comb. (See photos, p. 93.)

♦ You may use a Pet Hair Pic-Up (Helmac) adhesive roller, which is available at most pet stores.

If the health of your ferret is below par, chances are it will be reflected in the overall condition of your ferret's fur or whiskers.

WARNING SIGNS

♦ Excessive hair thinning and bald areas ♦ Short, broken whiskers ♦ Dry, brittle or dull hair coat ♦ Greasy hair coat on a neutered male ♦

Tails

Ferrets sometimes lose hair on their tails. It is common for the tail to take on the appearance of what we call a "rat tail", which may have scaly skin, blackheads and thin, bristly hair. Usually the hair grows back, the scaly skin clears up but the blackheads may remain.

Note that the cause of the condition is unknown but hair loss at the base of the tail or over the ferret's hind end also may be associated with adrenal disease. (See photo, p. 129.)

Fleas

How To De-Flea Your Ferret & Your Home (Do's & Don'ts)

If you keep your ferret clean and healthy, yet it keeps scratching itself, YOU probably will be scratching YOUR head wondering what's wrong.

Tommy Has An Itch

It may be nothing because scratching is normal. But, it may be a sign of fleas and/or flea bite dermatitis. To find out, use your fingers to separate the fur, slowly searching through, checking everywhere, especially under the chin, on the back, near the base of the tail, belly and inner thigh areas. Then comb through your ferret's coat with a flea comb. If you see little black specks of flea feces, it is a pretty good bet that your pet has a flea problem.

WHAT TO DO...
STEP 1 De-flea Your Ferret.
Read And Carefully Follow All The Label Instructions.

👍 USE a flea shampoo made specifically for cats or ferrets.

👍 STARTING at the head, shampoo the ferret from head to toe, including the tail. Do not get shampoo in the eyes, ears or nose.

👍 NEXT, using a flea comb, work the shampoo through the fur. The shampoo must remain on for at least 5 minutes to be effective.

👍 FINALLY, rinse completely and towel dry as you would after any bath, then check the coat again and pick off any remaining fleas.

WHAT NOT TO DO...

👎 Do not use products that are made for dogs only. They can be toxic for ferrets.

👎 Do not use flea products on ferrets UNDER 12 weeks of age. Use a regular shampoo safe for ferrets. Allow lather to remain on the ferret for at least 10 minutes. During that time use a flea comb and your fingernails to remove the fleas. Drop the temporarily paralyzed fleas into a cup of soapy water where they will drown.

👎 Do not use flea sprays, collars or dips on ferrets. They can be toxic!

👎 Do not put your ferret back into its environment until you have done everything in Steps 1 through 4 listed in this section.

☞ **NOTE** Fleas can be kept under control without resorting to dangerous pesticides. Safe and nontoxic alternatives are available. Ask your veterinarian for a recommendation.

Fleas are serious business. They live by sucking the blood from your pet. If your ferret gets even a moderate number of fleas and you do not treat the situation as soon as possible, YOUR PET COULD DEVELOP FLEA-INDUCED ANEMIA AND DIE.

STEP 2 De-Flea Your Ferret's Cage.

♦ REMOVE EVERYTHING from your pet's cage and wash thoroughly. Spray with a flea spray designed for cats and let dry.

♦ WASH all bedding and carpets, toys, dishes and water bottles in hot water. Machine-dry bedding on the maximum possible heat setting. Empty the litter pan, wash it, then add new litter.

STEP 3 De-Flea All Other Animals Living With You.

Follow the same steps as with the ferret.

STEP 4 De-Flea Your Home, Including Basements & Garages.

Your home MUST be treated by you or a professional exterminator because flea eggs, larvae and pupae are living and growing in the environment. Ask your veterinarian what he or she recommends.

☛ **WARNING** If you decide to use pesticides, all children and pets should be removed from the home BEFORE treatment. AFTER treatment, the home should not be occupied until the insecticide has dried and the house has been well ventilated for several hours.

If you use pesticide sprays, you should spray under furniture, carpeting, along baseboards, floor cracks, closets and bathrooms. Foggers also can be used: 6 oz. for small rooms, 12 oz. for larger rooms.

Read And Carefully Follow All The Label Instructions On Sprayers, Foggers, And Concentrates.

THE PROCESS...

- ♦ FIRST, vacuum the entire house. Then remove the vacuum bag, seal it with tape and throw it away!

- ♦ THEN wash all floors. Pay close attention to cleaning cracks and crevices.

- ♦ NEXT, turn off all air-conditioning and furnace systems and close windows.

- ♦ REMOVE all children and pets from the home.

- ♦ NOW treat your home. (You may want to wear a mask.)

- ♦ VACATE THE PREMISES.

- ♦ WHEN it is safe to return, open all windows to ventilate the house before children and pets are permitted to enter.

STEP 5 De-Flea The Outside Of Your Home, Including Dog Houses, Under Porches, Houses And Cars.

- ♦ FIRST, mow the lawn, rake and remove all debris.

- ♦ THEN treat the outside.

☞ ***WARNING*** WAIT until the treated area is dry before letting any children or pets play.

It is important to de-flea everything at the same time in order to be effective in getting rid of fleas. You will have to repeat this whole process in 10-14 days because new flea eggs will hatch. INTERRUPTING THE CYCLE IS THE KEY.

STEP 6 A Continuing Maintenance Program Is Necessary In Killing Fleas.

☞ **NOTE** If flea infestations are serious, it is recommended that you board your pets at a shelter or reputable boarding facility until the problem has been solved. Be sure to de-flea your pets prior to boarding and before you bring them home.

Ticks

Unfortunately, fleas will not be your only problem. Spring means the beginning of tick season. So be vigilant. If you live in an area where ticks are common, DO NOT keep your ferrets outdoors, in basements or garages unless you take precautions. Ticks are vampire-like little buggers that cause anemia and paralysis, which can result in the death of your ferret!

It is best to let your veterinarian remove ticks from your ferret. If your veterinarian is not available, you may try the following procedure:

You will need cotton swabs, alcohol, tweezers and an antiseptic such as Betadine (Purdue Frederick Company).

- ♦ Soak cotton swab in alcohol and saturate the tick.

- ♦ Use the tweezers to grasp the head of the tick as close to the skin surface as possible.

- ♦ Apply firm, steady traction and remove the tick. Be sure to kill the tick.

- ♦ Clean the area with the antiseptic.

- ♦ Then take the ferret to the veterinarian as soon as possible!

Chapter 8
FERRETS & THEIR FRIENDS

The Domesticated Ferret

One of the primary joys of living with domesticated ferrets is observing their natural behavior. (Read Chapter 1, All About Ferrets.) Seeing the world from a ferret's point of view magically will remind you to:

- make each day a new beginning

- make each moment a new adventure

- rejoice in life for life itself

- appreciate nature

- challenge life

- fight the odds and...

- take time to rest

It is important to understand the behavior of this domesticated species, its actions and interactions with other household pets and how it relates to its environment.

My First Ferret Experience

I purchased my first ferret Wheezee Girl from a pet store 7 years ago. She was happy, bright and curious. This little critter and I were totally devoted to one another for 3 years before I added another companion animal.

In May of 1992 I adopted a newly born kitten found on my girlfriend's doorstep by her husband. I volunteered to take the kitty, care for it until I could find it a good home.

I took the kitten home on a Friday night and to the veterinarian early Saturday morning. The doctor told me it was a boy, approximately 72 hours old and appeared healthy. After receiving all the necessary care and product information, I took him home and named him Bando Boy. Well, Wheezee and I fell in love with the kitten so the "good home" was our home.

Within a short period of time Bando started to crawl. Before long Wheezee and Bando were playing together. It was fun watching Bando trying to ferret his way under couches, bed blankets and inside dresser drawers. Bando could not quite understand why he was not able to do what Wheezee did.

When I was at home I would allow them to play together. But when I was away Wheezee was placed in her ferret "condo" for safekeeping. Bando would sleep in his bed beside her cage.

As time went by, Bando became territorial and rough with Wheezee; he wanted to "rule the roost". Respecting his boundaries, Wheezee had separate playtime with me.

Knowing how much Wheezee enjoyed having a companion, I adopted Pepper, a very dashing male ferret, about 1 year older than Wheezee, to keep her company. To prevent any antagonism, I put them in separate cages side by side to let them become acquainted. I supervised their playtime together as they sniffed the anal and neck areas of each other, allowing about 10 minutes before separating them.

I continued this twice a day, gradually extending their playtime until they became buddies. The technique worked so well that they eventually decided to become "roommates" in Wheezee's cage.

However, when I adopted a young female, Twiggy Silk, and tried the same process, it did not work. Wheezee tried to knock the daylights out of Twigg, and Pepper just ignored her.

I concluded that Pepper might tolerate baby Twiggy better and supervised them together at 10-20 minute intervals once a day for a month. The ploy worked, but when I tried to reintroduce Twigg and Wheezee, Wheezee reverted to fisticuffs again. Now she was jealous of Twiggy's friendship with Pepper. I did not give up. I started them at 5-minute intervals once a day and did manage to get my 2 girls to where they could be together for an hour before the fighting began. This went on for about 6 months.

One day, after a little over an hour of playtime, I noticed Wheezee going into Twigg's cage. This was something new. She had never done this before! I watched Wheezee eat Twiggy's food, drink her water, then go upstairs to the second level, get into Twiggy's sleepsack and go to sleep. I could not believe it! Totally amazed, I watched as Pepper followed, eating and drinking from Twiggy's dish and bottle. He went upstairs, got into Twigg's hammock, snuggled up and went to sleep. Needless to say, Twiggy wasn't far behind! She marched up to the second level and drove the two intruders out. It was hysterical to watch!

The next day, after about 2 hours of playtime, Twigg went back into her cage, ate, drank, then ran upstairs, crawled under her baby blanket, curled up and went to sleep. Then, along came Pepper and Wheezee. Once again they bypassed their cage, and this time the food and water. Pepper went to sleep in the downstairs hammock and Wheezee trotted upstairs, crawled under the baby blanket WITH Twigg and cuddled in. I sat there waiting for trouble. What a shock when nothing happened! I had never expected this turn of events. It was as though Wheezee and Pepper decided enough was enough. It was time to move house, and they began to live happily together. Of course, Wheezee and Twiggy still fought occasionally when they were out playing, but when they were at home they all cuddled up.

The Art Of Interaction

Playing cooperatively requires time. Animals, for the most part, live in the "I am" world: "I am the master of my domain". Territory is their first concern. Please do not expect social etiquette to be high on your pet's priority list.

Socializing does not come easily to some pets and sometimes it is hard to imagine that it will ever come at all. "Antisocial" behavior is normal to a pet that has had you and its domain all to itself.

In the beginning a great deal of the interaction will take the forms of hissing, neck grabbing, nipping or, in the case of a cat, scratching. Hopefully, there will be no biting.

For some time to come, there likely is to be a lot of what appears to be thoughtless and unkind behavior. The more aggressive pet(s) will try to establish dominance over the more submissive one.

Searching for the recipe for a peaceful home, I have found that the single-most important ingredient is understanding.

Ferrets With Ferrets

Ferrets that live in harmony with each other willingly share their cage, food, litter box, toys and human parents. As valuable as a playmate can be, compatibility will depend on the personality, energy level and age of each ferret.

The advantage of purchasing 2 kits that already have been cage mates is that these furry friends quickly can develop a strong bond between them. Of course, you will house 2 "babies", both requiring a lot of attention, training and constant supervision.

When considering a playmate for an aging ferret, it is wise to visit a ferret shelter to adopt a companion, which has been prescreened for temperament. Mature ferrets (2 years of age and older) usually have outgrown their terrible twos' stage. They share the same energy levels and usually are not interested in learning any new bad habits or throwing temper tantrums. Ferret shelters have ferrets of all ages.

Introducing A New Companion Animal

A new ferret will need to visit its veterinarian (experienced in ferret medicine) for a checkup and necessary vaccinations. Until then, restrict it from other pets, people and keep it inside your home.

You will need to create an area in your home where a new companion animal can establish its own domain. It takes time to adapt to a new home, new people, sights, smells, and new place to sleep, maybe even a new diet, not to mention other ferrets and household pets. Allow the newcomer to feel secure before it is introduced to the rest of the household pets.

THE INTRODUCTION PROCESS

Once your new pet has been given a clean bill of health by its veterinarian and has adapted to you and its new home, you may begin the introduction process.

The first encounter should be by placing the ferrets' cages side by side. In this way the ferrets have an opportunity to become acquainted through the cages. There may be fighting because ferrets can be territorial.

Keep the ferrets' playtime separate for a few days. When you feel the time is right, open both cage doors, stand back and let the little critters come out. The ferrets probably will sniff each other's neck and anal area, then get along or fight. Allow the initial contact to last for a few minutes. Do not push togetherness. Extend their social time slowly.

☞ **NOTE** If fighting occurs, distract your pets by squirting them with a water pistol; in this way, no one gets hurt. Or, wear heavy gloves and cautiously separate them. Do not hit the animals that are fighting; it creates fear. Once the fighting animals are apart, allow them separate space where they can run around without having a run-in. Time will tell if your pets can become friends.

The get-acquainted sessions should be brief and scheduled twice a day until the ferrets decide to become roommates. You will know when you see the two cuddle in their chosen cage. Friendship takes time. Some ferrets bond immediately, some within 2-3 months and, unfortunately, some never bond. If your ferrets do not bond after 6 months, a separate housing and playtime will be necessary. There are ferrets that will never accept another ferret.

Ferrets, Cats & Dogs

The advantage of having a kit (baby ferret) and a kitten is that the two can grow up together and possibly develop a strong bond.

As the kitten matures, it probably will not tolerate a nipping ferret. Sometimes ferrets outgrow the nipping stage by the age of 1. However, some ferrets will nip for attention, fun, or to say "I'm the boss" on occasion throughout their adult lives. Then again, some cats also nip for the same reasons. Supervision is recommended. Cats have been known to injure a nipping ferret. Ferrets have been known to injure kittens.

Puppies and adult dogs tend to tolerate an overly exuberant kit or adult ferret. However, dogs originally bred for hunting, by instinct, may kill a ferret. It is important that puppies and adult dogs be obedience-trained. Neutered animals usually are less aggressive, more gentle and easier to handle.

Ferrets and puppies or adult dogs will need guidance and, of course, constant supervision. Dogs have been known to kill ferrets.

THE INTRODUCTION PROCESS

Curious kittens or cats, puppies or dogs promptly will investigate a ferret through its cage. They often attempt to poke their noses or paws through the cage wire. However, this may be an opportunity for the ferret to take a nibble.

When you feel it is time for your cat or dog to meet your ferret, hold the ferret. (See photo, p. 113.) Be prepared to protect its face and body from a scratch or bite. All animals, no matter how gentle or sweet, can become territorial. Only you can determine when it is safe to allow your cat or dog freedom to study the ferret. (See NOTE, p. 111.)

As you soon will discover, some ferrets, cats and dogs need to be protected and separated from each other, at least at first. Provide a safe place to play. In households where there are multiple pets, introduce one pet at a time. Remember, kits, kittens and puppies are nonstop energy machines. Aging ferrets, cats and dogs may be set in their ways and may have a difficult time making friends with newcomers.

Ferrets love to steal the cat or dog food and stash it in hard-to-reach areas. You may leave the cat food but remove the dog food until the ferret is back in its cage. Ferrets should not be fed dog food and sometimes dogs are protective of their food.

A Ferret's Prey

Ferrets are among the smallest carnivores. They may be small but they can kill prey such as rabbits weighing many times a ferret's weight.

The most vulnerable household pets are rabbits, birds, mice, rats, hamsters, gerbils, guinea pigs and reptiles. If you have any of these pets in your home, proceed with caution where your ferret is concerned.

BOY MEETS GIRL

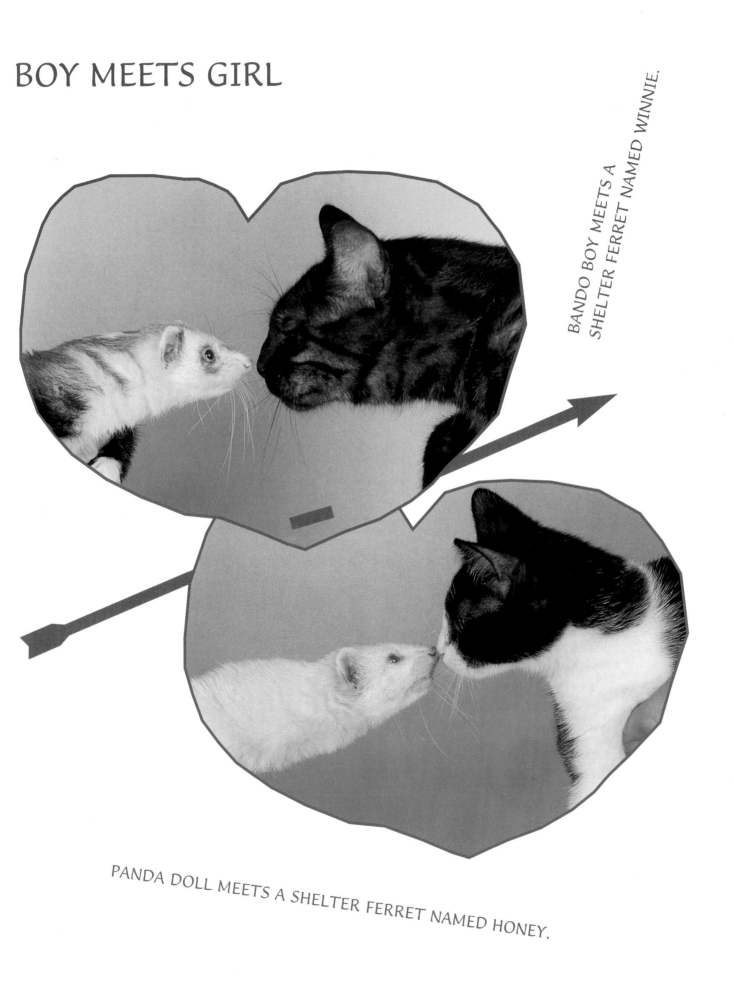

BANDO BOY MEETS A SHELTER FERRET NAMED WINNIE.

PANDA DOLL MEETS A SHELTER FERRET NAMED HONEY.

Chapter 9
TRAVEL PRECAUTIONS

The Strolling Ferret

Collar & Harness Training

Ferrets often are called the Houdini of the animal world and, no wonder, they are the ultimate escape artists! When a ferret DOES escape, you have a very slim chance of ever seeing it again. That is why it is so important for you to take precautions such as ferret-proofing (see p. 62) and using a cage when the animal is sleeping or when you are not at home. However, there are other preventive measures you can take.

When you take your ferret outside your home, you should use a ferret collar for identification purposes and a harness or travel carrier for safety.

👍 *A Ferret Collar*

One designed specifically for ferrets (including a name tag that has the ferret's name and your phone number) may be used when your ferret is playing outside its cage.

DO NOT USE a collar that can be stretched, such as nylon with elastic. A ferret will get it off. DO NOT USE a collar made of plastic. Ferrets will chew on and swallow plastic, causing gastrointestinal blockage and possible death. NEVER leave a collar on a ferret inside a cage. The animal could get caught on something and strangle itself trying to get loose. Ferrets that wear collars inside the house need to be supervised closely. Collars (especially with bells) can be the cause of a fatal accident if your pet gets wedged between two objects or caught inside a confined area.

👍 *A Harness*

The kind made especially for ferrets is best (including a name tag that has the ferret's name and your phone number). It should be securely strapped around the neck and body so that you can barely squeeze your pinkie finger through. Be careful not to squeeze the harness too tightly. NEVER leave a harness on inside a cage or inside your home. It should only be used for taking your ferret outside.

DO NOT USE a harness made from plastic. Ferrets will chew on and swallow plastic, causing gastrointestinal blockage and possible death.

NEVER WALK YOUR FERRET ON PAVED SURFACES (concrete, asphalt or brick) during hot weather. These hot surfaces will burn your ferret's delicate paws. I recommend leaving your ferret home on hot days.

NEVER TAKE YOUR FERRET TO THE BEACH. Ingested sand can cause gastrointestinal obstruction (impaction). Salt water can cause gastrointestinal problems and extreme brain edema. Ultraviolet rays may predispose the animal to retinal damage and skin cancer. And hot sand will burn your ferret's delicate paws.

NEVER PERMIT YOUR FERRET TO FROLIC AROUND IN SNOW FOR MORE THAN A FEW MINUTES. Ferrets' paw pads are delicate, similar to bare human feet. How long could you dance barefoot in the snow?

Training a ferret to wear a collar or a harness takes planning and patience.

Try This...

WAIT until your ferret has played for an hour or so and is starting to get tired.

TAKE it to a small, confined area such as a bathroom and try to put the collar or harness on. Your ferret probably will fight to get it off.

LEAVE the collar or harness on for only 3-5 minutes, supervising at all times.

REPEAT this procedure every day, extending the time slowly until the ferret finally accepts the collar or harness. You might try a little distraction with a new toy.

ADD a leash WHEN your ferret finally is used to the harness. Hold it so your pet can roam only as far as you want it to. NEVER TRY TO USE A LEASH WITH A COLLAR. The ferret simply will slip out of the collar and get away.

REPEAT this procedure with the leash about 5 minutes each time. Then remove it and put it away until your ferret goes outside with you.

☞ **NOTE** Do not be upset if this just won't work with your ferret. You may have one that absolutely will not accept a collar or harness. If you have tried this procedure and are still failing after 1-2 weeks, forget it, use a travel carrier when you take your ferret outside.

Tommy & Twinkle On Vacation

Traveling With Your Ferret

LONG TRIPS

If you are thinking about taking a trip outside your immediate area or state and want to take your ferret(s), you are going to have to do some preplanning and investigation first. (See p. 29, Are Ferrets Legal In The Area Or State In Which You Live?)

AIR TRAVEL

To Make Your Traveling Easier, Here Is A Quick Check List:

- ◆ Check the laws of the state or country you are going to visit. Find out if ferrets are legal. If traveling overseas, many countries demand that visiting pets be quarantined.

- ◆ Check with the airline about rules and regulations. Ask if pets are allowed in-cabin.

- Make a reservation for your pet. There is a charge for pets traveling in-cabin. Reconfirm your reservation 48 hours before flight. If your trip involves more than one airline, inquire how to transfer your pet from one airline to another. Be sure to plan adequate time.

- Take your ferret to the veterinarian for a physical examination, necessary vaccinations and medical certificates, which should include proof of a rabies vaccination.

- Tranquilizers are not recommended for your pets.

☞ **NOTE** Health certificates must be issued by an accredited veterinarian. You will need to know the expiration date of the health certificate.

Make sure you have an airline-approved travel carrier with an ID tag indicating your pet's name, your name, address and phone number. In addition, include the telephone number of a person who can be contacted at the destination about your pet should you be separated during travel. Display "Live Animals" labels on the case.

Whenever possible book a nonstop flight and avoid holiday or weekend travel. Morning or evening travel is most preferable during the summer, and midday flights are better during winter months. Ferrets are susceptible to heatstroke. (See Heatstroke, p. 141.)

FERRET ESSENTIALS DURING IN-CABIN FLIGHT:

Water Bottle
Remove before takeoff to avoid getting the ferret and bedding wet.

Food Dish & Dry Food
Feed a little at a time.

Blanket
For your ferret to curl up inside and sleep

Paper Towels Or Moist Towelettes

To clean up any mess it may make

A Favorite Toy

To help prevent boredom

Supplements

Such as Linatone for cats

First-Aid & Medicine Kit

☞ **CAUTION** ① It is best to carry your ferret in-cabin with you for its own protection. ② Ferrets that are extremely excitable, easily stressed, frail, sick or pregnant should not travel by plane.

LODGING

Providing your ferret is kept in a carrier or cage, most hotels and motels allow restrained pets. Ask when you make reservations.

Leaving Your Ferret Behind

Boarding your pet or hiring a pet-sitter can be an option if you decide to leave your pet behind. In either case, here are some tips:

♦ Ask your veterinarian, a local ferret shelter or another pet owner for a reputable boarding facility or pet-sitter.

♦ Be sure your pet is current on all vaccinations.

♦ Leave explicit instructions on feeding (a supply of your pet's regular food), exercise and safety routines.

♦ Make sure your ferret is housed in a suitable cage along with the appropriate housing necessities. (See pp. 45 & 48.)

♦ Leave phone numbers of your veterinarian's office, emergency numbers and where you can be reached. Make certain the pet-sitter clearly understands that should there be a medical problem of any kind, your pet must be taken directly to the veterinarian.

♦ Call your veterinarian and let him or her know who will be caring for your pet while you are away.

♦ If your pet is on medication, leave an ample supply along with clear, complete instructions.

♦ Request that the person(s) taking care of your pet ferret read this book in advance. Leave this book with the caretaker.

My experience with ferrets indicates they often become frightened, nervous, extremely excited or impatient when they are in unfamiliar surroundings. I prefer to leave my ferrets and cats at home with a reliable pet-sitter.

SHORT TRIPS

As I just mentioned, ferrets become stressed when outside their home environment. The only time I take my ferrets outside their home is when they are going to the veterinarian. As a matter of fact, the photographs in this book were taken at my home to avoid unnecessary stress for the ferrets.

Do not take your ferret out in public places for any extended period of time. Ferrets need to sleep 15-20 hours a day and must have access to food, water and a place to relieve themselves at all times. Do not take ill or aging ferrets to public places. It could cause negative influences on already weakened organs.

NEVER leave your ferret, or any pet, in a car with the windows rolled up. Even in the shade, the car quickly will become an oven and lead to fatal heatstroke. Remember, ferrets have a limited number of sweat glands and must stay cool!

☞ **NOTE** Do the following if you have to transport your ferret in hot weather and your car does not have air-conditioning. Always keep a couple of 2-liter soda bottles, filled 2/3 of the way with water in your freezer. Wrap one or two of the frozen soda bottles in a towel. Then place the wrapped bottles in the travel carrier with the ferret(s) or place on each side of the carrier to keep it cool.

Pets At Home Alone

Situation...

What would happen if you were involved in a serious accident and were unable to return home? Do you have an ID card in your wallet saying that you have pets at home alone, with specific instructions on whom to call in case of emergency? If not, here is what to do...

Place a visible ID card in your wallet that says... "In case of emergency, please notify (emergency contact)... And please remind them I have pets at home alone!"

The Emergency Contact Needs To Have The Following Information:

♦ Pet's name/type of animal

♦ Important behavioral traits

♦ Where pet food and supplies are kept

♦ Feeding instructions

♦ Medical information

♦ Veterinarian's name/address/phone

Make Copies Of This Information And...

♦ Keep one copy with your important papers.

♦ Place one copy with your emergency contact.

♦ Post a copy on your refrigerator (or someplace where it easily can be found).

♦ Leave this book where it can be seen and read.

Chapter 10
HEALTH CONCERNS

Twinkle & Her Veterinarian

Choosing a Veterinarian

A pet ferret's best friend is its veterinarian experienced in ferret medicine. Such a veterinarian provides you with accurate information regarding the unique health concerns of a ferret.

A veterinarian experienced in ferret medicine will know what to do in case of an emergency or a life-threatening disease. These veterinarians have developed a network of other practitioners who have experience with ferrets. They share and gain knowledge from each other about the latest treatments and techniques. A veterinarian who is not skilled in a particular area should be able to refer you to someone who is.

Protect the health and welfare of your ferret - choose a veterinarian experienced in ferret medicine.

Throughout your ferret's (or any pet's) life, veterinary attention will be needed. I encourage you to put money aside for routine and emergency care. Perhaps, a pet savings account.

Preventive Home Care

As a ferret owner you need to play an active role in the health of your pet. You need to take time daily to observe and become familiar with your pet's physical condition, behavior and habits.

By paying close attention, you will know when there is a need for prompt veterinary care. It is important to understand that ferrets, even with advancing disease, will try to carry on as usual. Their will to survive is strong.

Prevention does not mean simply "disease prevention". A ferret can risk illness, injury and even early death in many other ways. For example, ferrets can become disabled or die as a result of their investigative nature. Ferrets frequently get wedged between objects and can break or injure a limb trying to get loose. Dogs and cats teased by ferrets can bite and disable the ferret. Ferrets can die from eating household poisons. Motor vehicles can be a serious threat when ferrets escape from their home.

In all respects, you, the pet owner, are responsible for the risks this little investigator will take. Ferret-proofing becomes a significant factor in determining both the health and survival of your companion. (See Ferret-Proofing, p. 62.)

This chapter will help guide you through your pet's essential veterinary life-care program. It will help you understand the common health concerns of this very special pet and provide you with vital information should there be an emergency.

Preventive Veterinary Care

ANNUAL CHECKUP

Your ferret's first checkup is outlined in Chapter 3.

SECOND YEAR...

+ Physical: including ear, eye, mouth, abdomen, chest, skin and lymph node examination

+ Fecal (as needed)

+ Blood tests (as needed)

+ Vaccinations - canine distemper and rabies annual boosters

+ Teeth cleaning (as needed)

+ Heartworm prevention medication

When your ferret reaches 3 years of age, have your veterinarian do a thorough physical exam twice a year and laboratory work as recommended at least once a year.

The following tests will allow your veterinarian to diagnose early signs of disease and any other existing problems.

THIRD YEAR through OLD AGE...

This Complete Checkup Needs To Include:

+ Physical: including ear, eye, mouth, abdomen, chest, skin and lymph node examination every 6 months.

+ Complete blood cell count at least once a year.

+ Blood chemistries (including a fasting blood glucose) at least once a year.

+ X-rays (as recommended by your veterinarian).

+ Urinalysis (as needed).

+ Teeth cleaning (as needed).

Common Health Concerns

HEART PROBLEMS

The circulatory system includes the heart and blood vessels through which the blood flows. This system transports oxygen, nutrients and other vital materials to all areas of a ferret's body.

The hardest working muscle in your ferret's body is the heart. A ferret's resting heartbeat is a rapid 3-4 times per second, 180-220 beats per minute. This muscular pump is about the size of a grape and weighs only a few grams.

Ferrets can develop a number of heart conditions. The most common condition is cardiomyopathy (disease of the heart muscle).

HEART DISEASE WARNING SIGNS

Call your veterinarian if you notice any of the following signs.

♦ Weakness ♦ Labored or shallow breathing with or without wheezing ♦ Bubbling sound when the ferret breathes (congested lungs) ♦ Quick fatigue after exercise ♦ Lethargy, sleeps more ♦ Great difficulty in awakening from sleep ♦ Blue gums, tongue and paw pads ♦ Persistent coughing ♦ Loss of appetite ♦ Severe weight loss ♦ Fluid in abdomen (potbelly) ♦

RESPIRATORY INFECTIONS

The respiratory system (breathing system) includes the nose, sinuses, trachea, bronchi, lungs and related structures. This system supplies oxygen to the blood and rids the ferret's body of carbon dioxide (waste product).

A healthy ferret breathes between 33-36 breaths per minute. You may count this by watching the ferret's sides rise and fall.

A ferret's body temperature may range from 100°-103° F.

Tommy Has The Flu

Respiratory infections such as influenza, bronchitis and pneumonia can be caused by bacteria or airborne viruses, which are highly contagious. Viruses are transmitted to your ferret through human handling or contact with other animals and with inanimate objects such as litter boxes, food bowls and grooming tools. If you have a cold or the flu, wear a mask, and wash your hands before handling your ferret.

If any pet in the household exhibits respiratory signs, isolate the pet and take it to the veterinarian.

RESPIRATORY WARNING SIGNS

♦ Nasal discharge, sneezing, persistent coughing ♦ Body temperature above 103° F ♦ Loss of appetite ♦ Listlessness, weakness ♦ Rattling sound when breathing ♦ Difficulty breathing ♦ Persistent, rapid breathing ♦

☞ **NOTE** Pressure on the respiratory system caused by other factors such as tumors or fluid in the chest can cause similar respiratory warning signs.

Use a humidifier to help combat dryness in the ferret's living space and to help clear the ferret's nasal passages. It also is helpful to elevate the ferret's head to help it breathe easier.

CANCER

Cancer is the most common disease of ferrets in North America. Cancer in ferrets can be brought under control for an extended period or even cured if it is detected in time.

In many cases, treatment is available. The chance for a good result will depend on your ferret's general health, the type of cancer, location and the type of treatment used. The key is early diagnosis and treatment.

The most common ferret cancers identified are adrenal gland, insulinoma (pancreatic), lymphosarcoma and skin cancers.

ADRENAL GLAND CANCER

Your ferret has an adrenal gland located at the top of each kidney. These glands produce hormones that play an important role in controlling the body's response to physical and mental stress, keeping the body in balance.

Adrenal gland cancer causes one or both of the adrenal glands to produce more hormones and become enlarged.

ADRENAL GLAND DISEASE WARNING SIGNS

- Hair loss on the base of the ferret's tail, extending slowly throughout the body (See photos, p. 129.)

- Spayed female with swollen vulva, accompanied by discharge

- Flaky and red skin appearance

♦ Excessive scratching

♦ Change in personality such as aggression

♦ Mating behavior exhibited by spayed/neutered ferrets

♦ Difficulty urinating in male ferrets due to enlarged prostate

♦ Thinning and weakness of muscles

INSULINOMA (PANCREATIC CANCER)

The pancreas is a gland that is responsible for secreting the hormones insulin and glucagon, which play an important part in regulating the level of glucose (sugar) in the bloodstream.

Insulinoma is a tumor of the insulin-producing cells in the pancreas. These tumors cause an increased surge of insulin, which results in hypoglycemia (low blood sugar levels). Inappropriate insulin secretion will lead to the following potentially life-threatening signs:

INSULINOMA WARNING SIGNS

♦ Staring into space (disorientation) ♦ Drooling ♦ Gagging ♦ Pawing at the mouth (indicates nausea) ♦ Lethargy ♦ Depression ♦ Rear leg weakness ♦ Seizures ♦ Vocalization (whining, crying or screaming) ♦ Coma ♦

Note that the above warning signs are intermittent because the ferret's body will regulate itself with glucose as long as it can.

LYMPHOSARCOMA

The lymphatic system consists of lymph nodes and lymphatic vessels that are found throughout your ferret's body. This system helps regulate the fluid balance and immune system.

Lymphosarcoma or lymphoma is a malignant cancer of the lymphocytes, which may appear in any area of the ferret's body.

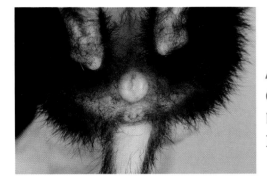

A SWOLLEN VULVA MAY BE A SIGN OF ADRENAL GLAND DISEASE, AN UNSPAYED FEMALE IN ESTRUS (HEAT), OR A FEMALE FERRET SPAYED INCOMPLETELY.

EARLY SIGNS OF ADRENAL GLAND DISEASE INCLUDE HAIR LOSS AT THE BASE OF THE TAIL.

EXCESSIVE HAIR LOSS DUE TO ADRENAL GLAND DISEASE

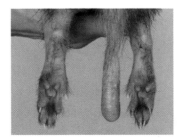

A SKIN TUMOR ON EYE AND TAIL

LYMPHOSARCOMA WARNING SIGNS

- ♦ Weight loss ♦ Lethargy ♦ Loss of appetite ♦ Labored breathing ♦

- ♦ Enlarged lymph nodes, which may be felt on each side of the ferret's neck and under the front legs, in front of the shoulders (armpit) and the inside of the rear legs (near the pelvis)

- ♦ Enlarged abdomen (indicating enlarged, internal organs such as liver or spleen)

SKIN TUMORS

The skin is the largest organ of the body and protects the internal parts from injury and disease-causing bacteria. Any change in the appearance of your ferret's skin may indicate a systemic problem.

The vast majority of skin tumors in ferrets are benign, however, all skin tumors should be removed because they are irritating to the ferret and some malignant skin tumors can spread within the skin and to other organs. The most common skin tumors are mast cell tumors and basal cell tumors.

SKIN TUMOR WARNING SIGNS

- ♦ Lumps in skin ♦ Raised, red or crusty areas ♦ Bleeding patches of skin ♦ Discolored patches of skin ♦

GASTROINTESTINAL DISORDERS

One of the most common gastrointestinal disorders seen in ferrets is gastrointestinal foreign bodies. Ferrets of all ages are famous for chewing on and ingesting a variety of foreign materials. You can help prevent this deadly disorder by following the simple instructions outlined in Toys, p. 52 and Ferret-proofing, p. 62 and Fur, p. 100.

Either a completely or partially blocked bowel is extremely dangerous. A blocked bowel requires immediate veterinary attention. Emergency surgery may be necessary. Death may occur in 24-48 hours if there is a complete intestinal obstruction.

GASTROINTESTINAL DISORDER WARNING SIGNS

♦ Vomiting ♦ Pawing at the mouth and salivating (indicating nausea) ♦ Dehydration ♦ Swelling of the abdomen ♦ Foreign objects in stool ♦ No stool for 12 hours or longer ♦ Black, tarry stool ♦ Loss of appetite ♦ Diarrhea ♦ Crying in pain when defecating ♦ Severe depression ♦ Collapse and coma ♦

EPIZOOTIC CATARRHAL ENTERITIS

Epizootic catarrhal enteritis (ECE), known by a variety of names such as "Green Diarrhea", "Green Slime", or "Mystery Disease", is an extremely contagious, diarrheal disease of ferrets, which was first seen on the East coast of the United States in March 1993. ECE is a suspected viral infection, which kills off the cells lining the small intestine. The loss of the intestinal lining markedly impairs the animal's ability to absorb water and food and also results in excessive fluid loss from the body in the form of green diarrhea. The green diarrhea simply is the bile coloring due to the rapid transit of this material through the intestine. Additionally, there is overgrowth of the intestinal cells, which secrete mucus, resulting in slimy stools.

ECE is passed in the feces of infected ferrets and recovered ferrets that show no clinical signs of the virus for up to 6 months or longer. The incubation time is approximately 2-3 days. ECE does not require direct ferret-to-ferret contact for transmission. The virus may be transmitted to a ferret from a person's hands, clothing, or even shoes.

ECE WARNING SIGNS

♦ Food refusal followed shortly by vomiting that is watery and may be mistaken for diarrhea if the ferret is not actually observed in the process

♦ Within a few hours, the ferret will begin to pass massive amounts of a watery forest-green colored stool in sudden, thin, swift streams, splattering everywhere. (Green-colored stool can be seen in other conditions.)

- "Birdseed stools", a sign of continued malabsorption

- Weight loss (Some animals continue to waste away for months, losing up to 50 percent of their body weight, and often never regaining their previous form.)

- Lethargy

The diarrhea can be rapidly dehydrating. Treatment for this disease is directed primarily at reversing the dehydration that accompanies the diarrhea, preventing a secondary bacterial infection in a host with an already stressed immune system, and trying to maintain as high a level of nutrition as possible in a severely damaged intestine.

Intravenous or subcutaneous fluid replacement may be administered by the veterinarian. An oral electrolyte solution such as Pedialyte (Abbott Laboratories) may be prescribed along with antibiotics.

A bland, highly digestible diet should be offered every 2-4 hours, as only a fraction of the nutrition that is taken is actually absorbed. Gerber's Second Foods Chicken is an excellent choice for a low-residue, highly digestible food. Many veterinarians recommend using other human products (Ensure or Sustacal) or Hill's Prescription a/d Diet specifically formulated for debilitated or recovering animals.

☞ **NOTE** Helping a ferret survive this viral disease requires dedicated home care. Ferret shelters such as The South Florida Ferret Club & Rescue, Florida, p. 163, The Ferret Association of Connecticut, p. 163, FAIR Shelter, Illinois, p. 164 and The Ferrets of Pet Pals, Virginia, p. 168, can provide you with home care information.

INTESTINAL PARASITES

Ferrets can develop diseases from parasites such as coccidia, giardia, roundworms, hookworms, tapeworms, flukes and toxoplasma. The most common parasites in ferrets are coccidia and giardia. These are microscopic, one-celled parasites that live in the intestinal tract. They are transmitted when infected animals shed the parasite in their feces.

FEEDING A SICK FERRET

A SICK FERRET NEEDS A NUTRITIOUS DIET.

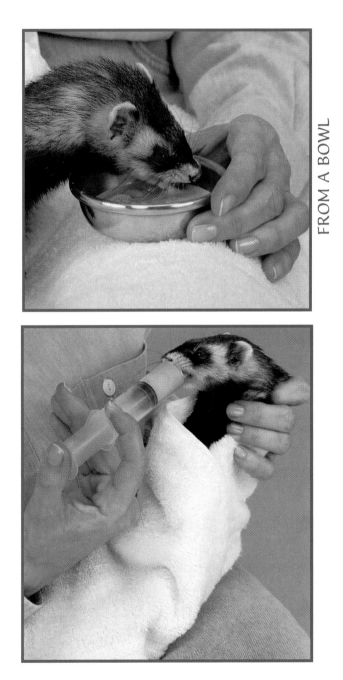

FROM A BOWL

FROM A FEEDING SYRINGE

Animals, which are stray, sold from breeding farms or at pet shops, are most at risk. They easily could be exposed to the contaminated feces of infected animals such as puppies, kittens or ferrets.

INTESTINAL PARASITIC WARNING SIGNS

♦ Soft, mucous-coated stool ♦ Diarrhea ♦ Bloody diarrhea ♦ Weight loss ♦ Poor coat quality ♦ Potbelly ♦ Weakness ♦ Lethargy ♦ Worms in stool ♦ Rice-like particles around the anus ♦

☞ **NOTE** If your pet has intestinal parasites, clean the litter box and the cage environment thoroughly each day and give fresh food and water. This will help prevent spreading and reinfestation. Keep all sick pets isolated. Keep your pets indoors.

Use medications prescribed by your veterinarian and have stool samples rechecked as requested. In most households with multiple ferrets, all ferrets will require treatment for intestinal parasites.

EYE PROBLEMS

Ferrets can be affected by eye disorders such as conjunctivitis, blocked oil glands along the lid, corneal lacerations or ulcerations.

If you notice any of the following warning signs, take your ferret to the veterinarian.

EYE DISEASE WARNING SIGNS

♦ White disk in the eye ♦ Cloudiness over surface of the eye ♦ Ferret bumping into walls or objects left about ♦ Ferret walking slower, hesitant to move about ♦ Bulging or swollen eyes ♦ Pus or crusting of the eyes ♦ Red, inflamed eyes ♦ Excessive tearing ♦ Brown staining around eyes ♦

BLINDNESS

Loss of eyesight in ferrets can be caused by various disorders such as cataracts, glaucoma, long-standing infections or eye injuries.

The ferret's sense of smell and hearing is much more acute than its eyesight. Blindness usually is tolerated well by the ferret. A blind ferret can live quite happily if given additional protection and special considerations.

Special Considerations For Blind Ferrets

- Keep ferret in familiar surroundings.
- Try to keep furniture in the same place.
- Do not leave children's toys on floor.
- Do not encourage the ferret to run quickly.
- Speak to your ferret when it is out of its cage.
- Speak to your ferret before you pick it up.
- Give lots and lots of affection.

Invent new sound, touch and smell games. Let the ferret win! Give your pet a treat when it wins. You can use sounds such as snapping your fingers, using a squeaky toy or saying its name many times. Encourage the ferret to follow the sound.

Ferret Dentistry

FRACTURED TEETH

Ferret dental problems are similar to dog and cat conditions. Fractured teeth occur commonly. A tooth can break during a fight or other trauma. At times only the enamel is chipped, which should be treated by allowing the veterinarian to sedate the ferret and grind down any rough edges. Other times the tooth fractures resulting in an exposed nerve. In this case, the tooth may appear discolored. If there is nerve exposure the treatment of choice is to remove the inflamed nerve to save the tooth. A metallic or acrylic material is used to restore the tooth.

A less-than-ideal method (but better than doing nothing) is to extract the tooth.

ORTHODONTIC CONDITIONS

Ferrets even suffer from some orthodontic conditions. One or both of the lower canines may abnormally point forward. This condition can cause the upper lip to become inflamed and result in excess dryness of the lower gum tissues. Treatment consists of removing half or three-quarters of the abnormal canine and sealing the pulp chamber with medication and material such as acrylic.

PERIODONTAL DISEASE

Periodontal disease is the most common dental condition in ferrets 6 years and older. Periodontal disease can be decreased through cleaning every 6 months and regular tooth brushing. Special dog and cat toothpastes appear to be safe to use in ferrets. Treatment of periodontal disease consists of extraction of loose teeth and frequent veterinary oral evaluation.

DENTAL DISEASE WARNING SIGNS

♦ Broken teeth ♦ Dramatic change of color in teeth ♦ Tartar build-up ♦ Ulcers along the gum or on the tongue ♦ Bright red gums ♦ Pale or white gums ♦ Red line on the gum margin ♦ Bad breath ♦ Difficulty eating ♦ Dropping food from mouth ♦ Inability to eat hard food ♦

CHECK YOUR FERRET'S TEETH AND GUMS FOR DENTAL DISEASE WARNING SIGNS LISTED ON PAGE 136.

MY TEETH NEED CLEANING.

Emergency First-Aid Kit

Keep your first-aid kit in a clearly labeled box and make sure its location is known to every caretaker of your pet. The supplies listed in this section have been suggested by my veterinarian. Ask your veterinarian what he or she recommends.

Pet Health Record

Maintain a complete health file on your pet in one location.

Emergency Phone Numbers

Veterinarian, emergency veterinary clinic and poison control center

Medications

Prescribed for your ferret by your veterinarian. Remove outdated medications.

A Feeding Syringe

May be used to give your ferret liquid or food when it is unable to drink or eat on its own. Ask your veterinarian or pharmacist about obtaining feeding syringes.

Karo Syrup, Honey Or Nutri-Cal (EVSCO Pharmaceuticals)

For low blood sugar - mix a 4:1 solution of water and Karo Syrup, water and honey or water and Nutri-Cal. For example: 4 parts water to 1 part Karo Syrup. You also may use Gatorade undiluted. Put into feeding syringe, then coax your ferret to drink it. This should not be used as a treat. Use only as an emergency measure. Excessive use of sugar can lead to diabetes.

Cat Hairball Laxative

This may be used as a hairball remedy or to help prevent an obstruction, as mentioned in TOY WARNINGS, p. 54.

Eye Wash

Ideal for flushing out eyes

Topical Antiseptic Such As Betadine

For cleaning wounds and sores

Anti-Bacterial Skin Ointments

To soothe minor rashes and burns

Bandage Material

Gauze, sterile pads and adhesive tape

Styptic Powder

For nail-cutting accidents

Rectal Thermometer

Digital thermometers are easier to read. Your ferret's body temperature should not rise above 103° F or fall below 100° F.

Petroleum Jelly

For taking temperatures rectally or to help relieve paw pad dryness

Miscellaneous Items

Towels, cotton swabs, soap, scissors, tweezers, nail clippers, pen light or flashlight, ice pack, heating pad and latex gloves

Emergency First Aid

First aid is not a substitute for veterinary treatment. However, knowing some first-aid basics could help save your pet's life.

Immediately take an animal to the veterinarian following first-aid attempts.

WOUNDS & BLEEDING

Clean wounds with cold water, then wrap the affected area with a sterile gauze bandage or a clean cloth. Apply direct pressure to the bandage to stop the bleeding. If bleeding persists, add more bandage and increase the pressure. Do not remove the original bandage because you could disturb any clotting that has begun. Avoid tight bandages that could cut off circulation. Immediately take the animal to the veterinarian.

BURNS

Without delay flush the burn area with large amounts of cold water. Apply an ice pack for 5-10 minutes. Immediately take the animal to the veterinarian.

EYE INJURIES

For scratches and burns flush with a steady stream of room-temperature water. Cover eye with gauze pad. Keep your pet in a semi-reclining position. Never apply any medications. Immediately take the animal to the veterinarian.

Do not attempt to remove foreign objects from the eye. Do not apply pressure. Immediately take the animal to the veterinarian.

FRACTURES

Do not try to set a fracture. Handle the ferret carefully and keep it immobilized by gently wrapping a towel around it. Immediately take the animal to the veterinarian.

SHOCK

Shock occurs when the body tries to conserve the blood to vital internal organs. Shock can occur as a result of or after illness, serious injury or fright. Shock can be fatal. Cover your pet with a towel or blanket. (Leave head uncovered.) Keep your pet quiet in a warm, dry area. Immediately call your veterinarian.

SHOCK WARNING SIGNS

♦ Shivering ♦ Pale skin and grayish gums ♦ Rapid, weak pulse ♦ Shallow and or rapid breathing ♦ Weakness ♦ Vomiting ♦ Diarrhea ♦

SEIZURES

A seizure usually lasts 1-3 minutes and occurs when there is an abnormal electrical impulse in the brain. The symptoms of a seizure include: uncontrolled, jerking movements, salivating, defecating, urinating and vocalization (whining, crying or screaming).

The most common cause of seizures in ferrets is hypoglycemia (low blood sugar) due to insulinoma. Other causes include: poison, severe ear mites, head trauma or severe liver disease.

Do not put yourself at risk by restraining the ferret (or any pet) during a seizure, but do make sure the ferret is in a safe place. If you have to move your pet, gently use a towel and wrap it loosely around the ferret. Time the seizure.

Ferrets, like other animals, do not swallow their tongues. Do not put your finger in its mouth, you will get bitten.

After the seizure, keep your pet calm, quiet and cool. Rub a drop or two of honey and water or Karo syrup and water on the ferret's gums every 5 minutes until the ferret responds. It usually takes 15-30 minutes to recover from the seizure. As soon as your ferret has recovered, feed it a soft, high protein diet from a feeding syringe to stabilize its blood sugar level. (See Supplemental Diet Suggestions, p. 151.) Immediately call the veterinarian.

HEATSTROKE - FATAL WITHIN MINUTES!

ALWAYS provide your ferret with fresh water and keep it in a cool temperature setting. Lack of water and prolonged exposure to temperatures more than 80° F (27° C) will lead to heatstroke.

WARNING SIGNS

♦ Open-mouthed breathing ♦ Panting ♦ Mucus from mouth and nose ♦ Toepads becoming bright red then turning purple to blue ♦ Limpness ♦ Seizures ♦ Collapse ♦

Temperature Above 80°

If any of the preceding should happen, immediately cool the animal by applying a cool (not cold) wet cloth over its legs, paws, hindquarters and tail. Or, immerse the ferret in room temperature or lukewarm (not cold) water, keeping the head above the water.

If your ferret already has collapsed, DO NOT GIVE IT ANY LIQUID BY MOUTH! If it responds well to the wet cloth, mix a 4:1 solution of Karo Syrup and water, honey and water or Nutri-Cal (EVSCO Pharmaceuticals) and water. You also may use Gatorade undiluted. Put ONE of the mixtures in a feeding syringe and put a DROP OR TWO at a time ON OR UNDER THE TONGUE. Try coaxing your ferret to drink it. IMMEDIATELY CALL YOUR VETERINARIAN because fluids may need to be injected subcutaneously (beneath the skin) or intravenously (into the veins). Other medications may need to be given to combat shock. Oxygen also may need to be administered.

☞ **NOTE** If you are in a situation where the temperature is too hot for your ferret, you can keep it cool by: ① always having water available; ferrets need more water in warmer temperatures, ② giving it a pan of water to play in (Change it hourly to keep it cool.) or ③ spraying your ferret with a cool mist.

☠ ACCIDENTAL POISONING

☞ **WARNING** Do not give your ferret any human or animal over-the-counter or prescription medications unless directed by a veterinarian. Ask the veterinarian how much, how often and for how long to give the drug. IT IS EASY TO OVERDOSE A FERRET.

If your pet gets into any kind of medication, chemicals or cleaning products, immediately contact your veterinarian and/or the National Animal Poison Control Center listed below. The control center's veterinarian will recommend a specific course of action. If your ferret gets coated with something toxic, immediately give it a bath.

National Animal Poison Control Center (NAPCC)
900-680-0000 ($20 first 5 minutes, $2.95 each additional minute will be billed to your phone number) or call: **800-548-2423** ($30 per case, credit card only)

Have this information ready. They will ask the following questions:
♦ species? (ferret-polecat family)
♦ sex, age, weight?
♦ spayed/neutered?
♦ signs?
♦ amount of poison ingested?
♦ chemical name of the poison? (Read the label for ingredients.)
♦ how & when was your pet exposed?

Pets & Allergies

Allergies are reactions to a substance or "allergen". Allergies in ferrets can be triggered by flea saliva, certain foods, environmental irritants such as dust, pollens, smoke, perfume, kitty litters, aromatic oils (pine and cedar chip shavings) and chemical substances in drugs.

Allergic reactions can be serious for your pet. If you notice any of the following warning signs, take your pet to the veterinarian.

WARNING SIGNS

♦ Excessive itching ♦ Sneezing ♦ Nasal discharge ♦ Hacking cough ♦ Excessive tear production ♦ Difficulty breathing ♦ Clear or blood-tinged vomit ♦ Skin inflammation ♦ Swollen, reddened paws ♦ Scaliness of skin ♦ Hair loss ♦ Skin sores ♦ Bloody diarrhea ♦ Weakness ♦ Collapse ♦

Both animals and humans suffer from similar allergies. Sometimes we have allergic reactions to our pets, which often cause allergic symptoms such as sneezing, itchy and watery eyes and a stuffy nose. Other times an allergic reaction can lead to a more serious problem such as asthma.

Here Are Some Suggestions To Help You Combat Allergens.

♦ You can clean the air in your home by purchasing HEPA filter air cleaners and electrostatic air cleaners. These cleaners eliminate smoke, odors, fumes, dander, chemicals and almost all airborne dust particles.

♦ Use a high-efficiency vacuum cleaner or bag to remove dander from carpeting, drapes and walls.

♦ Remove the carpeting or use carpet treatments such as an anti-allergen dust spray, which is an anti-dust mite and anti-dander carpet spray.

- Do not allow your pet in the bedroom and especially do not allow your pet to sleep in bed with you.

- Wash your pet every 2 weeks to remove the dander build-up on fur.

- Do not smoke around your pets. Cigarette smoke not only is harmful but can predispose an animal to allergies.

For environmentally safe products, locate an allergy supply store near you. Or, call the National Allergy Supply Inc. at 800-522-1448 and ask for the Allergy Relief catalog.

Preparing A Ferret For Surgery

In being the "provider of all things" to our pets, we need to assume the responsibility of helping them cope with temporary changes in their lifestyle such as surgery.

Surgery is unnatural for pets but I have learned that reassurance, comfort and a sense of security for your pet will go a long way in helping it recover.

Sick ferrets do require a lot of extra special attention. Here are my suggestions to help you help your ferret.

- Learn everything you can about your pet's condition. Knowing what to expect will help lessen the worry and the stress.

- The day before the surgery prepare your ferret by cutting its nails, cleaning its ears and bathing it (if needed).

- Prepare a quiet, resting place for your pet to recover from surgery, away from other pets, people, loud noises and other distractions.

- Prepare an isolation cage. (See photo, p. 148.)

- Stock the necessary supplies needed for your ferret's recovery such as: bottled water, a supplemental diet, a feeding syringe, paper towels or first-aid supplies.

♦ Ask your veterinarian what medications will be needed by your ferret after surgery. Purchase them ahead of time, if possible. Find out if medication should be given before, with or after feedings. Ask about possible side effects.

☞ **NOTE** Your ferret will be required to fast before surgery. If the veterinarian requests that you bring your ferret in the early morning hours, ask what time the ferret is scheduled for surgery. Take the food and water away *no longer than 6 hours before* and tell the veterinarian the time of your ferret's last meal.

AFTER-SURGERY HOME CARE

The first 48 hours will be an uncomfortable time for you and your ferret. The first week after surgery is a crucial healing time. The healing process is slower in aging ferrets. Here are some suggestions to help you and your ferret.

♦ If you can, plan to take time off, so you can be with your pet, especially the first 24-48 hours.

♦ Arrive at the clinic a few minutes early to pick your pet up to avoid feeling rushed.

♦ Bring a pen and paper to write down the veterinarian's instructions regarding medications, surgery precautions and home care. Each surgery has its own precautions. Make sure you find out whom to call after hours in case of an emergency.

♦ Bring a travel carrier equipped with a baby blanket to keep your ferret warm. Ferrets are susceptible to hypothermia after surgery. In addition, you may want to bring a heating pad. Plug it in at the clinic on a low setting to warm the baby blanket. When the veterinarian hands you your ferret, wrap the heated blanket around your pet. Place the pet in its carrier.

♦ Go directly home, place your delicate, little critter in the isolation cage to keep your recovering pet from being active.

- Slightly elevate your pet's head (to help your ferret breathe easier), place a warm blanket or towel over its body. Heat blankets or towels in the clothes dryer. Allow your ferret to rest but check on it every hour or two to make sure that your pet is comfortable.

- When your ferret wakes up, gently pat its head and talk to it. Feeling a gentle touch and hearing a reassuring tone of voice (TLC) will go a long way in helping your pet recover.

- Give your pet some fluids and a small amount of food. (Read Feeding A Sick Ferret, p. 149.)

- Check the incision site at least twice a day. Pets sometimes lick, chew or scratch on the incision during the healing process. (The healing process causes itching.) If the incision appears swollen, red or is seeping fluids or pus, immediately call your veterinarian.

Within a day or so, you will notice that your ferret probably will want to get out of its cage. When your ferret appears energetic and with its veterinarian's permission, allow the ferret to move about outside its cage in a small, confined area. When it appears tired, return your ferret to its recovery cage for safekeeping.

If you have other ferrets or other household companions, allow them to visit with your recovering pet through its isolation cage for short periods of time. Moving around the isolation cage is good for the ferret because limited exercise will stimulate circulation, help relieve constipation (common after surgery), improve your ferret's attitude and speed recovery.

☞ **NOTE** Ferrets may have a delayed hair regrowth after surgery depending on the time of the year. And sometimes coat color or texture may change. The skin may turn a bluish or olive color.

You may place your ferret back in its ferret "condo" (suitable cage) when the veterinarian gives you permission to do so.

ISOLATION CAGE FOR A SICK FERRET

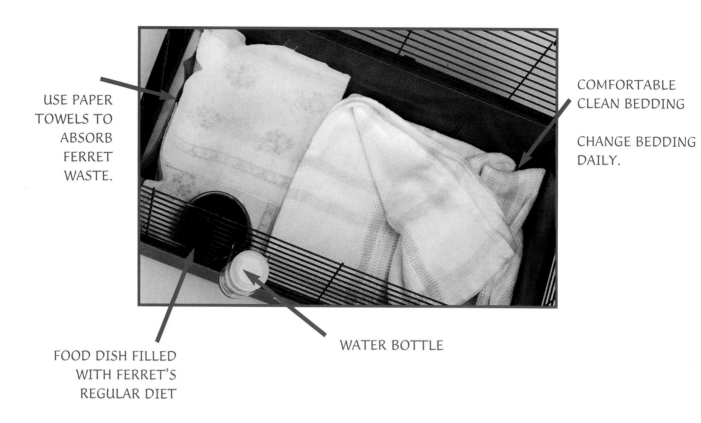

USE PAPER TOWELS TO ABSORB FERRET WASTE.

COMFORTABLE CLEAN BEDDING

CHANGE BEDDING DAILY.

FOOD DISH FILLED WITH FERRET'S REGULAR DIET

WATER BOTTLE

PEPPER KISSING HIS WHEEZEE GIRL IN HER ISOLATION CAGE DURING HER RECOVERY FROM SURGERY

Feeding A Sick Ferret

Sick ferrets may have a poor appetite and may not eat well on their own. Because a ferret's body is working hard to recuperate from illness or surgery, it must have more fluids than usual to prevent dehydration and a high caloric intake of nutritious food to fuel its recovery.

FLUIDS

Fluids are necessary. Oral electrolyte solutions such as Pedialyte or Gatorade often are recommended. Fluids can be mixed with food or given alone in between feedings.

Ferrets too sick to drink on their own must be encouraged to drink with your help. (See photos, "Feeding A Sick Ferret", p. 133.) Follow these simple instructions:

♦ Prepare fluids in a feeding syringe.

♦ Place the ferret in your lap, gently scruff the back of its neck and use the other hand to give it fluid.

♦ Drop a little fluid into the corner of its mouth. Allow the ferret to swallow. Continue giving small amounts of fluid until the ferret spits it out. This is an indication that the ferret has had enough.

♦ Give fluids frequently throughout each day until the ferret is drinking on its own.

☞ **NOTE** If your ferret has had surgery the anesthesia initially may leave your pet nauseated causing it to vomit. When the ferret has stopped vomiting, you may attempt to give fluids. However, if the vomiting is persistent, call the veterinarian.

If the ferret refuses fluids, call the veterinarian. Your ferret may need to be given fluids subcutaneously (beneath the skin) or intravenously (into the veins).

NUTRITIOUS FOOD

Prepare a supplemental diet (one suggested by your veterinarian). You may either try feeding the ferret from a small bowl, spoon or a feeding syringe. (See photos, "Feeding A Sick Ferret", p. 133.)

♦ Place a towel on your lap or wrap a towel around your ferret to catch food spills.

♦ Place the ferret in your lap. If using a feeding syringe, gently scruff the back of the ferret's neck. Use the other hand to feed your ferret.

♦ GENTLY SQUEEZE A SMALL AMOUNT OF FOOD from the syringe into the corner of the ferret's mouth. After the ferret has swallowed, continue giving it small amounts of food (allowing it to swallow each time) until the ferret spits it out. This is an indication that the ferret has had enough.

♦ Feed small amounts of food at least every 3 hours during the day until the ferret is eating full meals on its own.

♦ Place a water bottle and its regular food in an isolation cage. The ferret may nibble when it begins to feel better. (See photo, "Isolation Cage", p. 148.)

A SUPPLEMENTAL DIET

Ill and convalescent ferrets often require a soft diet. How often and how much food they consume depend on the circumstances surrounding the ferret's illness.

If your ferret is ill and having difficulty eating, ask your veterinarian what to do. WITH YOUR VETERINARIAN'S PERMISSION, you may want to try one of the following supplemental foods until your ferret is able to return to its regular diet. Different diseases and medications may require special dietary regimes.

SUPPLEMENTAL FOODS ARE NOT MEANT TO BE FED TO YOUR FERRET FOR AN EXTENDED PERIOD OF TIME. EVENTUALLY, THE ANIMAL SHOULD BE WEANED FROM THE SOFT-FOOD DIET AND BACK TO ITS REGULAR DRY FOOD.

In order to feed a soft diet through a feeding syringe, the foods need to be liquefied (all lumps removed). Heat the soft diet by placing the small container of food or syringe in a bowl of hot tap water for 5-10 minutes. Do not use the microwave. Heating this way results in dangerous hot spots, burning the ferret's mouth, tongue and throat.

THE FOLLOWING FOODS MAY BE FED SEPARATELY OR BLENDED TOGETHER. KEEP ALL UNUSED PORTIONS REFRIGERATED AND USE WITHIN 48 HOURS. SERVE THE SOFT DIET WARM.

Supplemental Diet Suggestions
- 1/2 c. (4 ounces) a/d (a prescription diet by Hill's, available through your veterinarian) **or**

- 1 jar Gerber 2nd foods such as chicken or turkey **or**

- 1/2 c. premium ferret food such as the Totally Ferret diet soaked in enough water to cover and soften completely

Optional
- 2 oz. Ensure (vanilla) (Abbott Laboratories) or Sustacal (vanilla) (Mead Johnson), a nutritionally complete liquid food, ready to use and lactose-free can be mixed with any of the above foods.

These foods, mixed with a little warm water and blended thoroughly, easily may be fed from a small bowl or put into a feeding syringe and fed to your ferret several times a day. You may add medication, if needed. When your ferret is feeling better, slowly add its regular dry food (crushed) to the soft diet. Start out with a little and gradually add more and more regular food to make it thicker and drier.

The above foods also may be added as a supplement to aid thin ferrets in gaining weight.

Chapter 11
REMEMBERING
WHEEZEE & PEPPER

WHEEZEE

Once upon a time there was a little white "ferret princess" named "Wheezee." She was blessed with exceptional beauty, intelligence and an inner radiance that touched my soul and rekindled my relationship with animals.

This is our story.

It all began about 7 years ago with a trip to the pet store on behalf of my 3 goldfish. As I walked into the store I noticed a small cage on the floor near the door. Sitting in that cage on a bed of cedar chips was a black-eyed, white animal that I had never seen before. I asked the storekeeper what it was and she told me it was a 6-month-old female ferret left there on consignment. I had no idea what a ferret was but I immediately was drawn to her. When I bent down for a closer look, the ferret seemed to reach out to me. Being allergic to animals, I was hesitant at first but when those big, black eyes gazed into mine, I could not resist.

I sat on the floor next to her and got permission to open the cage and pick her up. Within 5 seconds the ferret jumped out of my arms and leaped about the store in an energetic fashion. I tried to catch her but she quickly disappeared under a stack of cages, then reappeared on the other side, reverting to leaping about. To my surprise she came chuckling over to me, nipped my ankles and ran about my feet. I quickly scooped her up and cuddled her.

After an hour of playing with this irresistible, little critter, I noticed that I did not appear to be allergic. So $95 later, she was mine! I decided to name her Wheezee because she did not make me wheeze.

Unfortunately, the storekeeper knew very little about ferrets or their care, nor did she have any reading materials to give me, so my new-found friend and I were on our own, unprepared for the road that lay ahead.

Totally devoted to being a good ferret parent, I decided that Wheezee and I (the girls) would go shopping and buy everything she needed. Four pet stores and 3 hours later we were pooped. I had purchased everything recommended by every pet store.

Arriving home I had 4 ferret books, scoopable litter, a litter box, dry cat food, liver dog treats, a small cage, cedar chips for bedding, a plastic food and water dish and 8 latex toys.

I quickly put everything together and put Wheezee in her cage to rest. However, she did not rest. Wheezee tipped over her food and water into her cedar chip bedding and burrowed into the scoopable litter creating quite a mess all over her, the cage and floor. She then began sneezing and coughing. I did not know what to do. I took her out of the cage, cleaned her up and carried her to my bed. Wheezee quickly ferreted her way under the blanket and went to sleep. I placed more food and water next to the bed and scattered newspaper about the room for her to poop and pee on. I closed the bedroom door and crawled in bed next to her.

Watching her sleep I decided to read at least two of my new ferret books. The information in the second book contradicted the information in the first book. I would not dare open the third book. I knew that a good night's sleep was what I needed because figuring all of this out was going to require energy.

The next morning was spent feeding Wheezee, giving her a bath and cleaning up her business from about the room. Next, I threw out the litter, cedar chips and the awful tasting liver dog treats that Wheezee spit out. Wheezee had no desire to go back in that small cage so I put it away.

Having to be at work, I left Wheezee in my bedroom with food and water and gave her the 8 latex toys to play with, closed the door and went off to work.

Arriving home late that evening, I found my little girl collapsed on the floor with bits of latex everywhere. In a panic I got the Yellow Pages, found an emergency veterinary hospital and quickly drove her there. Wheezee had eaten 50% of a latex toy. With immediate attention and proper veterinary care her life was saved.

With this near tragic incident came a promise to Wheezee. I would make every effort to learn everything I could to take care of my girl.

And so my research began and my journey with Wheezee continued...

I spent many days on the telephone tracking down a veterinarian experienced in ferret medicine, ferret shelters, other ferret owners and still more and more books. It would have been so much easier if I'd had one accurate, up-to-date and easy-to-understand reference guide.

The first 6 months were the most joyful of times, and yet the most trying. I was an inexperienced ferret owner searching for answers. Wheezee was going through the terrible two's and then one morning I awoke to a potentially life-threatening asthma attack.

I had developed an allergy to Wheezee, but I was determined to keep her. With immediate attention by an asthma and allergy specialist and by purchasing the necessary allergy relief supplies, my condition soon was under control.

Wheezee and I were inseparable. We shared many happy moments together. I found myself wanting to finish my day and rush home to see her. As soon as I arrived home, Wheezee would start pacing in her cage waiting for companionship.

My Wheezee grew more precious with each passing year. Into our fourth year together my work schedule was consuming more of my time. And I noticed that Wheezee sometimes was lonely and bored. I decided to get Wheezee an additional companion. Perhaps a boyfriend.

PEPPER

It was now time to visit the South Florida Ferret Shelter. I was introduced to a 4-year-old male ferret named Pepper, who had been rescued from the streets of Fort Lauderdale, Florida. He was healthy, handsome and very charming.

The perfect companion for my "Little Princess", Pepper was Wheezee's "Knight in Shining Armor".

Wheezee and I were both pleased. Wheezee began to dance and chuckle like never before. It was fun watching them explore, play and cuddle.

Pepper was such a pleasure and adapted so nicely that within 6 months I decided to adopt another.

TWIGGY

One day I was called upon by the South Florida Ferret Shelter to rescue an unwanted ferret. Arriving at the address, I was given a box covered with a net. Inside was a sad sight. The dark sable ferret looked like a skeleton covered with fur. She had been fed a diet of lettuce, tomato and crab meat.

I took the frail, little animal and put her in my travel carrier and by the time I arrived at the shelter, she had captured my heart. I named her Twiggy Silk and got permission from the shelter to adopt and care for her.

With medical care, nutritious food and TLC, Twiggy blossomed into a rambunctious, little character. I call her my wild child. She is forever in trouble. She climbs, stashes the cat's food, gets herself caught in between or inside objects at least once a week; steals whatever she can carry; loves to nip my ankles, then runs away. Yet, she has used the litter box from day one and gives me many kisses. I often just sit in amazement watching Twigg do "her thing."

WHEEZEE & PEPPER

As Wheezee turned 4, I noticed symmetrical hair loss around the base of her tail. I took her to the veterinarian (experienced in ferret medicine). After performing a thorough examination the veterinarian suggested Wheezee probably was showing signs of adrenal gland disease. The doctor recommended exploratory surgery and I agreed.

In November 1993 surgery was performed. The diagnosis was adrenal gland cancer and insulinoma. With appropriate medical care, lots of TLC and quiet isolation, Wheezee recovered from surgery.

The veterinarian had removed Wheezee's left adrenal gland and some of the tumors on her pancreas. I was informed by the veterinarian that Wheezee still could lead a happy life for at least 1 1/2-2 years.

In July 1994 Pepper also began showing signs of adrenal gland disease and insulinoma. Exploratory surgery was performed. The diagnosis was confirmed.

Pepper's condition was more advanced than Wheezee's. His life expectancy after surgery was only 6 months.

As long as Wheezee and Pepper were eating and playing, I would do whatever possible to make their lives comfortable.

In December of 1994 Wheezee and Pepper began to rapidly deteriorate and I knew that soon I would have to make the dreaded decision. I thought about it for days as I watched Wheezee and Pepper give every waking moment their all.

The mere thought of not seeing them in their cage when I woke up each day was painful. It was not easy to accept the fact that their life as I knew it was almost over. And then again, they were only 5 1/2 and 6 1/2 years of age.

EUTHANASIA

I had decided that when Wheezee and Pepper no longer were enjoying life, I would end their pain by euthanasia. However, that was the logical decision. Emotionally I was not doing so well.

I had made the appointment twice, and twice I canceled. In January of 1995 I truly knew their days were numbered. I was now suffering with them. I made the third appointment for January 10 at 6:00p.m. I arrived at the clinic at 5:30p.m. I was led into a private room where Linda Knowles-Lord, D.V.M., was waiting. I quietly spread their baby blankets on an examination table. There were no words, just sadness. I took Pepper out of his cage first. I kissed him and he kissed me. I told him that I loved him and that I would miss him dearly. I then held him and through my tears I watched as he was euthanized. I bent down and kissed him and gently stroked his body as he died. As I choked back the tears I stood there for a moment. I took a deep breath and then took Wheezee from her cage. I felt overwhelmed as I kissed her and she kissed me. I held her gently and then put her on the table. I stood there in disbelief for a few moments and then the pain of this moment took over. As I wrapped Wheezee and Pepper in their favorite baby blanket I looked up at Dr. Lord who also was crying. She had recently euthanized her dog, Lysse. It was a difficult time for us both. We shared our feelings for a while. Dr. Lord's compassionate nature and humane hand were comforting.

I left through the back door and drove home. I carried their bodies inside the house. I sat in the dining room holding them for about 30 minutes before I had the courage to put them in cold storage until I could let go and bury them.

TWIGGY'S REACTION

I went to the cage where Twiggy was sleeping. I decided not to bother her until morning.

I went to bed but I could not sleep. So finally I got up. Twiggy was awake. I took her out and held her for a long time. I told her that Wheezee and Pepper had died. I promised to take good care of her.

Twiggy searched the entire house for Wheezee and Pepper several times that day. She would not eat or drink. I tried giving her her favorite treat but she refused.

The next day Twiggy repeated the same behavior. I was depressed and so was Twiggy.

The third day I took Wheezee and Pepper over to Pet Heaven Memorial Park where they would be buried in the pet cemetery. I picked out their gravesite, a casket, ordered their headstone and left them there. The funeral was planned for Saturday, January 14, 1995.

THE BURIAL

Twiggy still was depressed so I decided to take her to the funeral. Twiggy and I arrived Saturday at 9:30a.m. The staff who worked at Pet Heaven Memorial Park were wonderful, understanding and very caring. As I entered the viewing room where Wheezee and Pepper were laid out in their casket, Twiggy frantically started pacing in her carrier. I took her out of the carrier and held her securely, allowing her to get next to the casket. But that was not good enough. Twigg wanted to touch them. Her wish was granted. When her tiny nose and paw touched Wheezee and Pepper, she quickly pulled away. I feel that it was then she knew that they were gone and not just hiding in some yet-to-be-discovered place.

I held her close and said a few words to Wheezee and Pepper. I placed Twiggy back in her carrier. I folded the satin cover over Wheezee and Pepper and placed a rose beside them. The casket was sealed. I carried the casket and Twiggy to the grave site. I placed Twigg in her carrier, next to the grave. I carefully put the casket in the ground, placed flowers and sprinkled some earth onto the casket. I took Twiggy out of her carrier and holding her we watched as Wheezee and Pepper were buried.

Twiggy and I returned home. I held her, put her in her cage and laid down on a blanket on the floor beside her. We both were emotionally exhausted.

The next morning Twiggy and I ate breakfast together. Twiggy began eating normally that day but did not dance. Within 2 weeks she was introduced to her new companion, "Newfy", adopted from the South Florida Ferret Shelter. Newfy was housed in a separate cage. Within 1 month Twiggy allowed Newfy to move in. Twigg and Newfy are the best of buddies but she is the boss.

WHEEZEE AND PEPPER

♥

WHEEZEE & PEPPER
FOREVER FRIENDS
B — 7 — 13

I will carry in my thoughts

Their joy
Their companionship
Their unconditional love
Their funtimes
Their exploring times
Their significant moments
Their pain
Their courage
Their strenghts
Their limitations
Their final moments

Wheezee and Pepper are with me always

Chapter 12
FERRET CONNECTIONS

For information regarding national ferret organizations or on starting a shelter, contact Pamela T. Grant at (703) 354-5073.

For information regarding Ferret Friends Disaster Response International, contact Chere McCoy (407) 567-0994, FAX (407) 562-5696. The group is a growing organization that helps ferrets involved in natural disasters.

CANADA

The Friends & Ferrets
Tracey Lee Rein
Delta, B.C.
(604) 943-8149

The Friends & Ferrets
Sheena Staples
Vancouver, B.C.
(604) 299-0255

Ottawa Ferret Assoc.
Peggy Clarke
Ottawa, Ont.
(613) 258-6134

UNITED STATES

ALABAMA

Gulfcoast Ferret Rescue
Mrs. Marty Loeffler
Chickasaw, AL
(334) 457-8346

ARIZONA

Central Arizona Ferret Club
Suzanne Resinger
Phoenix, AZ
(602) 840-0813

Heartbeat Ferret Shelter
Helen White/Dan McCullough
Phoenix, AZ
(602) 547-0016

Curious Critters
Lori & Bob Schultz
Glendale, AZ
(602) 843-4056

Ferret Friends
Ginny Childs
Tucson, AZ
(520) 622-4940

CALIFORNIA

Ferrets Anonymous
Pat Wright
San Diego, CA
(619) 497-1084

California Domestic Ferret Association
Hildy Langewis
Castro Valley, CA
(510) 357-4938

California Domestic Ferret Association
Jeannie Carley
Woodside, CA
(415) 851-3750

COLORADO

Colorado Ferret Rescue
R. A. Yaroush
Niwot, CO
(303) 444-7364

Ferret Rescue of
Western States
Carolyn Kinsey
Pueblo, CO
(719) 391-2627

Colorado Ferret Rescue
Scotti Pelham
Littleton, CO
(303) 972-3316

Ferrets Etc.
Stephanie Sheme
Engelwood, CO
(303) 761-1983

Ferret Information
Mary Mayday
Aurora, CO
(303) 690-1759

CONNECTICUT

Ferret Association of
CT Halfway House
Ann & Vanessa Gruden
Hartford, CT
(203) 247-1275/ 247-9129

DELAWARE

Delaware Valley Ferret Rescue
C. Sooy
Newark, DE
(302) 738-0115

Dream Catcher Ferrets
Steve Krouse
Wilmington, DE
(302) 633-1090

FLORIDA

Ferret Information
Stevie Rutter
Jacksonville, FL
(904) 398-9691

Ferret Information/Rescue
Barbara Ludt
Green Cove Springs, FL
(904) 284-9232

Ferret Information
Carol & Richard Hill
Micanopy, FL
(904) 466-4098

Gainesville Ferret Meisters
Club & Rescue
Newberry, FL
(904) 332-4357
(904) 377-1382

Falkor Ferrets
Gayle Parker
Gainesville, FL
(904) 377-0848

Foxtrot Ferrets
Charlene Terry
Branford, FL
(904) 935-2833

Ferret Information
Mary Lou Simpson
Osteen, FL
(407) 321-9188

Central FL Ferret Friends
Debbie Coburn
Orlando, FL
(407) 380-8712

Brevard Ferret Lovers
Brevard County
(407) 725-0335
Seminole County
(407) 696-0917

Ferret Friends of Indian River
County (FFIRC)
Chere McCoy
Vero Beach, FL
(407) 567-0994

South FL Ferret
Club & Rescue
Angela Espinet
Miami, FL
(305) 251-8647

Suncoast Weasel
Waystation Shelter
Barbara & Steven Boyce
St. Petersburg, FL
(813) 541-4918

Ferret Connection
Marylou Johnson
Ft. Myers Beach, FL
(941) 466-8900

GEORGIA

Georgia Domestic
Ferret Association
Jan Lovell
Cumming, GA
(770) 442-5917

Information & Rescue
Ginney Laut
Cleveland, GA
(706) 865-7734

Fantastic Ferrets
Elizabeth Ann
Talmo, GA
(770) 534-1976

For The Love Of Ferrets
Julie Todd
Blairsville, GA
(706) 745-3965

ILLINOIS

Greater Chicago
Ferret Association
Norman Stilson
Westchester, IL
(708) 442-8650

FAIR Shelter
Mary Van Dahm
Westmont, IL
(708) 968-3189

Central Illinois
Friends of Ferrets Rescue
Kathy Fritz
Champaign, IL
(217) 356-6063

Peoria Area
Ferret Connection
Mary Oyer
Morton, IL
(309) 263-7603

INDIANA

Far Fetched Ferrets
Dan Thomas
Elkhart, IN
(219) 296-1711

Ferret Information
Kathy Ohlrogge
New Whiteland, IN
(317) 535-8010

IOWA

Ferret Park
Todd Herriott
Mike York
Ames, IA
(515) 233-5131

Ferret Information
Dr. Jean Fitzgerald
Wellman, IA
(319) 646-6028

Eastern IA Ferret Assoc.
Suzanne Hoofnagle
West Branch, IA
(319) 643-7429

KANSAS

Ferret Family Services
Troy Lynn Eckart
Manhattan, KS
(913) 456-8337

LOUISIANA

Ferret Information
M & M Forsythe
Franklin, LA
(318) 828-5904

MAINE

Mainely Mustelids Shelter
Lynn Hendrickson
Brunswick, ME
(207) 725-5978

MARYLAND

AFA
American Ferret
Association
Frederick, MD
(301) 898-3228

Howard County Ferret Rescue
Lucia & David Ditch
Laurel, MD
(301) 776-8841

Fur Thieves of the Heart
Nelda & Dave Clark
Ft. Meade, MD
(410) 674-5053

Fairytail Ferrets Rescue
Chip & Chris Gallo
Rockville, MD
(301) 424-0199

Shadyside Ferrets Rescue
Ellen Byrne
Germantown, MD
(301) 540-2756

Metro Friends Ferrets
Denise Edens
Germantown, MD
(301) 972-1618

All About Bandit
Carol & Jim Scott
Crownsville, MD
(410) 923-2417

Sanders Halfway House
Judith Sanders
Linthicum Heights, MD
(410) 850-0143

Baltimore Ferret Club
Diane Rogers
Baltimore, MD
(410) 448-1281

Prehistoric Ferret Rescue
Chrissy Cappelluti
Frederick, MD
(301) 694-0393

Halfway House
Diana Bachman
Hagerstown, MD
(301) 790 2560

Fran's Ferret Rescue
Fran Wiles
Smithsburg, MD
(301) 416-0606

Carroll County
Ferret Rescue
Joyce & Terry Fike
Taneytown, MD
(410) 751-1526

Shady Hollow Ferretry
Sally Heber
Thurmont, MD
(301) 898-3228

MASSACHUSETTS

Massachusett's Friends of the Domestic Ferret
Sharon Burbine
Bill Williamson
Wakefield, MA
(617) 224-1098

United Ferret Organization
Bruce White
Assonet, MA
(508) 644-5562

MICHIGAN

Ferret Information
Vickie Glendening
Lincoln Park, MI
(313) 383-7902

Great Lakes Ferret Assoc.
Gloria Davis
Grosse Ile, MI
(313) 676-9138

Checker Farms Ferrets
Micki Wingate
Maybee, MI
(313) 587-3959

Ferret Information
Debbie Miller
Taylor, MI
(313) 287-4572

Ferret Information
Paul Rahman
Wayne, MI
(313) 782-4293

Ferret Information
Karolyn Maher
Redford, MI
(313) 534-0297

Ferret Information
Carolyn Distell
Pontiac, MI
(810) 253-9692

Ferret Information
Carol & Kermit Kranz
Auburn, MI
(517) 662-4169

Wind Haven Farm Shelter
Russell Miller
Greenville, MI
(616) 754-7695

Ferret Information
Michaele or Mark Beaton
Grand Rapids, MI
(616) 363-6539

Ferret Information
Stacey & Daniel Platzer
Vicksburg, MI
(616) 649-4266

The Ferret Inn
Debi Arthur
Lansing, MI
(517) 484-4024

MINNESOTA

Ferret Information
Joel Johnson
St. Paul, MN
(612) 433-5993

Ferret Information
Randy Sellers
St. Paul, MN
(612) 731-2550

MN Ferret Association
Katie Loween
Wyoming, MN
(612) 462-5597

MISSISSIPPI

Ferret Rescue
John Pummill
Southaven, MS
(601) 393-7717

Wreaking Crew Shelter
Wade Montes
Ocean Springs, MS
(601) 875-8927

MISSOURI

Ferret Referral & Rescue
Leah & Jim Harrington
Jennings, MO
(314) 382-6327

K.C. Ferret Hot Line
Bobbi McCanse
Kansas City, MO
(816) 842-3707

MONTANA

Elizabeth & Jim Neff
Hamilton, MT
(406) 363-6333

NEBRASKA

Ferret News/Club
Lee Donehower
Omaha, NE
(402) 573-1064

Carwin's Rescue
Pat Butcher
La Vista, NE
(402) 331-3015

NEVADA

Club & Rescue
Kris Lissner
Incline Village, NV
(702) 831-8571

NEW HAMPSHIRE

Four Lil' Paws Ferret
Joan & Dick Bossart
Merrimack, NH
(603) 424-2941

Ferret Services of Freedom
Stephanie Mudgett
Freedom, NH
(603) 539-5631

Ferret Wise Rescue
Alicia & Dino Drakiotes
Marlborough, NH
(603) 876-4975

The Ferret Rescue
Linda Phaneuf
East Hampstead, NH
(603) 329-5367

Tri-State Frisky Ferrets
Thrica Conley
Nashua, NH
(603) 598-1209

NEW JERSEY

*Northwest Jersey
Ferret Rescue*
Jane Casale
Ogdensburg, NJ
(201) 827-5170

Ferret Lifeline Rescue
Ellen Demchak
Wantage, NJ
(201) 702-0553

Ferret Information
Beth Klein
Little Ferry, NJ
(201) 440-8501

Ferret Information
Patty Krywos
Westwood, NJ
(201) 664-4781

Friends of Ferrets Shelter
Carolyne & Peter Koch
Mercerville, NJ
(609) 586-9526

Hamilton Ferret Rescue
Sandy Stilwell
Hamilton Square, NJ
(609) 586-6962

Itty Bitty Critter Rescue
Nancy & Rich Joyce
Toms River, NJ
(908) 341-6960

NEW YORK

Big Apple Ferrets
Sue Morrow & Neal Segal
New York, NY
1-800-FERRET 2
(212) 388-8652

*N.Y. Ferret's Rights
Advocacy*
David Guthartz
Oceanside, NY
(516) 536-6615

Ferret Rescue
Gale Putt
Setauket, NY
(516) 689-6420

Concerned Ferret Owners
Carol Levy
Tupper Lake, NY
(518) 359-7998

Little Thieves Rescue
Thomas Ievoli
Kings Park, NY
(516) 269-7236

Modern Ferret Magazine
Mary & Eric Shefferman
Massapequa Park, NY
(516) 799-1364

*Woodland Sprite
Ferret Rescue*
Patricia Savoie
Amsterdam, NY
(518) 842-3820

Ferret Halfway House
Richard Smith
Queensbury, NY
(518) 793-0147

Central NY Ferret Friends
Otto Christofferson
Liverpool, NY
(315) 457-1746

The Ferret Rescue Center
Vera Kellog
West Monroe, NY
(315) 623-7490

Elvenoak Ferretry
Amy Sipher & Peter Ladd
Syracuse, NY
(315) 424-8849

Obadiah's Ferret Shelter
Patricia Northnagle
Brockport, NY
(716) 637-4589

Ferrets & Friends of NY
Jeanne Stadtmiller
Hilton, NY
(716) 637-0898

WNYFLFA
Deborah Riccio
Rochester, NY
(716) 473-7292

NORTH CAROLINA

Ferret Information
Lee Anne & Gary Newsom
Gibsonville, NC
(910) 697-7540

North Carolina Ferret Assoc.
Joan & John Armshaw
Elon College, NC
(910) 342-7748

Critter Care Shelter
Vicki Waldren
Pollocksville, NC
(919) 224-0663

Ferret Rescue of Boone
Jeff Collier
Boone, NC
(704) 265-1513

Guardian Angel
Linda Goodwin
Apex, NC
(919) 362-8460

OHIO

Ferret Sense/Shelter
Linda Harrah
Buckeye Lake, OH
(614) 929-3392

Friends of Ferrets Shelter
Kim & Joe Burian
Sagamore Hills, OH
(216) 467-2837

MASKeteers
Michelle Poehler
Warren, OH
(216) 369-4947

Friendly Ferrets
Debbie Scott
Ripley, OH
(513) 392-9302

Ferret's Dream House
Lori Sies
Cincinnati, OH
(513) 733-8167

OKLAHOMA

Save Our Critters
Debbie Smith
Altus, OK
(405) 563-2681

OREGON

Oregon Ferret Association
Christine & David Mathis
Portland, OR
(503) 557-8369

PENNSYLVANIA

FFC
Ferret Fanciers Club
Mary Fields
Pittsburgh, PA
(412) 322-1161

The Ferret Connection
Tracy McAlister
Stewartstown, PA
(717) 993-9484

PA Ferret Association
Janice Moore
North Huntington, PA
(412) 863-5125

Central PA Ferret Rescue
Kymberlie Becker
State College, PA
(814) 867-8562

Susquehanna Valley Ferret Club
Beth Ann Lee
Highspire, PA
(717) 939-0625

Starfire's Ferret Shelter
Jodi & Steve Schroth
Harrisburg, PA
(717) 540-1078

Halfway House
Charlynn Lockard
Williamsport, PA
(717) 322-2802

The Blue Mountain Ferret
Beth Schwenk
New Ringgold, PA
(717) 943-7683

Lehigh Valley Ferret Club
Judy & Jerry Benner
Catasauqua, PA
(610) 266-7189

Legion of Superferrets
Rose Smith
Levittown, PA
(215) 946-2747

Ferret Rescue of Delaware Co.
Sandee Chreiman
Upper Darby, PA
(610) 352-4852

Oxford Ferret Shelter
Samantha Vulliet-Benson
Oxford, PA
(610) 932-5463

The Ferret Gallery
Cheryl & Christopher Goedeke
Harleysville, PA
(215) 256-1164

Montgomery Ferret Rescue
Desiree Kehr
Hatfield, PA
(215) 368-3906

Ferret Paws Rescue
Donna & Warren Olsen
Hatfield, PA
(215) 855-5167

Warmfuzzy Ferret Rescue
Shirley Hertzog
Fleetwood, PA
(610) 926-9087

The Ferret Lady
Betty J. Jones
Fountainville, PA
(215) 249-1064

RHODE ISLAND

Ferret Association of RI
Holly & Moe Cyr
North Kingstown, RI
(401) 294-6309

TENNESSEE

TN Valley Rescue & Club
Gina & Bobby Eaton
Soddy Daisy, TN
(423) 843-1786

Ferret Awareness Club
Mary Geiger
Bristol, TN
(423) 764-1095

Bumblefoots Ferretry
Betsy Hultin
Cosby, TN
(423) 436-2183

Ferret Rescue
Lorie Frezza
Memphis, TN
(901) 794-3035

TEXAS

Beggars & Thieves Ferrets
Patricia Israelson
Plano, TX
(214) 424-5262

Ferret Information
Linda Lowder
Anna, TX
(214) 752-5401

Carealot Ferrets
Nadine Hindman
Longview, TX
(903) 643-9420

Ferret Information
Eva McClung
Longview, TX
(903) 643-9389

Ferret Lovers Club of Texas
Karen Grant
Bedford, TX
(817) 577-3949

For The Love of Ferrets
Jimena Humme
League City, TX
(713) 332-4948

The Weasel Waystation
Ann Holman
Bryan, TX
(409) 589-2870

SAFE
Candi & Rick White
San Antonio, TX
(210) 661-9195

Schermerhorn's Shelter
Sharon Schermerhorn
Austin, TX
(512) 453-8597

UTAH

UFA Ferret Shelter
Bridget Bollard
Draper, UT
(801) 571-2903

The Utah Ferret Association
Sam & Matthew Ouimette
Taylorsville, UT
(801) 269-1181

VIRGINIA

STAR* Ferrets
Shelters That Adopt
& Rescue Ferrets
Springfield, VA
(703) 354-5073

LIFE
League of Independent
Ferret Enthusiasts
Burke, VA
(703) 913-1115

The Ferrets of Pet Pals
Pam & John Grant
Annandale, VA
(703) 354-5073

ACME Ferret Company
Ann Davis
Burke, VA
(703) 913-1115

Rodejo Ferrets Rescue
Debra & Ron Johnson
Falls Church, VA
(703) 534-0160

LAFF
Louden Area Ferret
Fanciers Club
Vickie McKimmey
Leesburg, VA
(703) 777-2112

Halfway House for Ferrets
Lynn Reid
Reston, VA
(703) 860-4965

Ferret Information
Ava McDannell
Herndon, VA
(703) 476-4834

Silhouette Ferrets
Louise Knott
McLean, VA
(703) 356-8151

Mount Vernon Ferrets
Joya & David Lane
Manassas, VA
(703) 330-0484

Infinity Ferrets
Carol Keith
Sterling, VA
(703) 430-6329

Zen & The Art of Ferrets
Diane & Bill Killian
Woodbridge, VA
(703) 590-3473

North American
Ferret Association
Lucy & Chuck Skaggs
Dale City, VA
(703) 590-2132

Ferret Information
Meg Carpenter
Alexandria, VA
(703) 765-4353

Ferret Rescue of Tidewater
Beverly Vautrinot
Chesapeake, VA
(804) 545-3715

Dragon Run Ferrets Rescue
Georgia Bailey
Newport News, VA
(804) 887-5688

Ferret Information
Ann & Robert Martin
Lynchburg, VA
(804) 845-4417

WASHINGTON

Ferrets NW - Seattle
Edward Lipinski
Mercer Island, WA
(206) 232-1228

Ferrets NW - Bellingham
Dr. T. & C. Metour
Bellingham, WA
(206) 599-2514

Ferrets NW - Everett
Lorelei Seifert
Mukilteo, WA
(206) 353-1037

Ferrets NW - Tacoma
Bobbie & Monty Younce
Tacoma, WA
(206) 584-5266

Los of Washington
Sharon Bowman
Bremerton, WA
(206) 792-1387

Ferret Club
Joe Chevere
Silverdale, WA
(206) 697-4524

WEST VIRGINIA

Ferret Information
Chris & Chip Gallo
Harpers Ferry, WV
(304) 728-1180

Happy Hollow Farms
Shirley Myer
Lost Creek, WV
(304) 884-7058

WISCONSIN

Ferret Foundlings Shelter
Karen Yaremkowych
Horicon, WI
(414) 485-2512

Ferret Fanciers of
Greater Milwaukee
Judy Vowell
Milwaukee, WI
(414) 535-1523

Central Wisconsin
Ferret Fanciers
Cher Dunerson
Wausau, WI
(715) 675-6939

WYOMING

Frazzled Ferret Rescue
Ann Clark
Sheridan, WY
(307) 674-4349

Closing Words

Seven years ago I could not have imagined the transformation in my thinking and behavior, which resulted from my journey with my first ferret Wheezee. That journey has changed my life, and it is my intense hope that *A Practical Guide To Ferret Care* will help change yours.

As a child, I often used to say to myself, "When I grow up and have my own home, I will have lots of pets." As the years went by, I developed allergies to animals and lost the vision. I slowly forgot the impact that animals had in my childhood. But fortunately, I met and fell in love with a little white ferret, which helped me renew that vision. Wheezee made a difference in my life. Certainly, all of my pets have changed the way I see the world. I cannot imagine life without the joy of animal companionship.

Whether your enjoyment or involvement with animals is as profound an experience as mine, I encourage you to see the world through the eyes of your pet and embrace this innocent life. Domesticated animals are treasured gifts and they offer many rewards. Please always remember that animals have feelings and needs. They need loving homes and security in order to thrive. They need to know they matter.

In my day-to-day experiences with domesticated pets I often am reminded that it is not pets that need training, but rather humans. My goal in writing *A Practical Guide To Ferret Care* is to improve the lives of the domesticated ferret, and ultimately, all pets. The misery we all have seen in neglected and abused pets is an unforgivable malice that cannot continue. The world does not belong to human beings alone but to all living things. Human/pet relationships can be mutually and harmoniously inclusive.

An informed and caring pet owner can return a pet's love by providing those elements that are simple but fundamental to all living things - understanding, love and protection - but most importantly, your pet needs your unconditional willingness to be a part of its life.

Ferrets Inc. would like to hear from you. To be included on our comprehensive mailing list, please send your name, address and phone number to:

Deborah Jeans
c/o Ferrets Inc.
P.O. Box 450099
Miami, FL 33245-0099

References

Anderson, Nina & Peiper, Howard. "Are You Poisoning Your Pets?" Connecticut: Safe Goods, 1995.

Bell, D.V.M., Judith A. "The Pet Ferret Owner's Manual." New York: Christopher Maggio Studio Inc. & Miracle Workers, 1995.

Campbell, Karen L. "*Principles of Flea Control in the Environment.*" Veterinary Practice Staff. Volume 3, Issue 2, March/April 1991

Caras, Roger A., "Do You Care What Happens to This Dog?" ASPCA (The American Society for the Prevention of Cruelty to Animals) Newsletter, 1995.

Eisenberg, Arlene & Murkoff, Heidi E. & Hathaway, B.S.N., Sandee E. "What To Expect-The Toddler Years." New York: Workman Publishing, 1994.

Fox, J. *Biology and Diseases of the Ferret.* Philadelphia: Lea & Febiger, 1988.

King, Carolyn. *The Natural History of Weasels & Stoats.* Ithaca: Christopher Helm Ltd. and Cornell University Press, 1989.

MacDonald, Dr. David, "The Encyclopedia of Mammals." New York: Facts on File Inc., 1984.

Pane, D.V.M., Robert T. "*Ask the Vet...Can I Take My Ferret To The Beach?*" The Miami Ferret Club Inc., Ferret Footnotes, Volume 1, Winter 1991.

Sommerstein, Alan H., The Comedies of Aristophanes: "Acharnians", Vol.1. England: Aris & Phillips LTD, 1980.

Winsted, Wendy. "Ferrets". Hong Kong: T.F.H. Publications Inc., 1983.

Index

Ferret Notes